Walking Through Honey

Also by Brian Sherman

The Lives of Brian: Entrepreneur, Philanthropist, Animal Activist
(Written with AM Jonson)

Walking Through Honey

My Journey with Parkinson's Disease

Brian Sherman
with AM Jonson

Artworks by Brian Sherman
Multiple exposure composite photographs by Gary Grealy

Brian Sherman's movement therapy (Brian playing table tennis at home), multiple exposure composite photograph by Gary Grealy

*To my wife Gene, my children Emile and Ondine,
and to Caroline and Dror, who have become my children.*

*To my grandsons and granddaughter, Milo,
Zachary and Cy, Jasmine, Dov and Lev.*

First published in 2022 by Noble Books
Unit E1, 3-29 Birnie Avenue
Lidcombe NSW 2141 Australia

Publishing services by Noble Books

Text copyright © Brian Sherman, 2021
Interviews © Sherman family, Dr Stephen Tisch, 2021
Walking Through Honey – The Video Series © Rod Freedman, 2021
Artworks © Brian Sherman, 2020, 2021
Photographs © Gary Grealy, 2021

All rights reserved. The author asserts their moral rights in this work throughout the world without waiver. No part of this book may be reproduced, or stored in a retrieval system, or transmitted in any form or by any means, electronic, mechanical, photocopying, recording, or otherwise, without express written permission of the publisher. For information about permission to reproduce selections from this book, write to editions@booktopia.com.au.

ISBN 9781922598820

Published in Australia and New Zealand for Brian Sherman by
Noble Books, an imprint of Booktopia Group Ltd

Cover photograph: Gary Grealy © Gary Grealy: Brian Sherman's movement therapy (Brian walking at slow and medium pace), multiple exposure composite photograph
Cover and text design by Daniel New, danielnew.com.au
Edited by Bernadette Foley, broadcastbooks.com.au
Typeset in Minion Pro 11pt by Daniel New
Printed by Peachy Print, Sydney, peachyprint.com.au

Foreword

Jeffrey Masson

I have always had a fondness for beautiful objects that are entirely natural: a rock that reveals an opal inside before it is polished; a piece of driftwood that has not been carved; a cone that has fallen from a tree. The book you are holding in your hands is such a natural gem. Brian has not polished his narrative; he is not trying to persuade you of anything. He has no agenda beyond telling you the unvarnished truth. It is the story of his Parkinson's as he has lived it and continues to live it. It is a deep glimpse into a world that is very hard to describe, especially by someone who is inside that world, looking out, and increasingly is unable to articulate what it feels like in ordinary conversation. But Brian does exactly that in this remarkable book. He explains what it really is like to suffer the ravages of Parkinson's disease.

Brian is a person used to success. Many people in Australia know who he is, and what he has achieved. What people do not necessarily know, though, is that Brian reached the heights without losing something very precious: kindness. I remember, not all that long ago, sitting in Brian's office at Voiceless and expressing my wonder at the fact that I had never heard him raise his voice or even express anger.

'Do you ever feel angry, Brian?' I asked.

'Actually, no, I don't,' he said.

I cannot think of anyone else I know who does not experience anger, but Brian, I am sure, is telling the truth. I have not seen him yell, or be unkind, or humiliate anyone. For a man at the top of his profession, that is unusual. But it goes along with something very deep in Brian: the ability to feel the pain of others.

Brian is incapable of observing the suffering of others without feeling pain himself. And by 'others' I include all animals, and not just the human animal. This is why Brian co-founded Voiceless, one of the premier animal rights organisations in the world, with his daughter Ondine. When Brian describes seeing a baby pig who is soon going to be slaughtered, he says, 'Sorry, mate, that this has to happen to you. I look into your eyes and I see a being, just like me. It pains me more than I can say that you must suffer this fate. It makes no sense to me.' How many titans of industry could look at a simple pig on her way to the killing floor, and say these deep words that resonate with so many people? He must be unique.

And so this disease, which takes away his voice (but not his mind), seems completely unfair. Of course, that can be said of any disease. Each person, as Brian points out, wants to shake their fist at God and ask, 'Why me?' To which the famous (or infamous!) answer is, 'Why not you?' But God's response is not entirely fair, nor does it satisfy Brian. And I side with Brian here. Surely we can do better than simply shrug and say, 'That is life.'

And this is precisely what Brian does not do in this book. He does not shrug off his own experience. He tells you, from the very beginning, what it feels like to have Parkinson's. He remembers everything, and so do those around him, who add their own perspective on what he has had to go through. We are with him when he starts to notice that not all is well in his movements and his stamina.

Brian was unstoppable. What happened? How could this happen? He tries to answer this and he is far more successful than a long line of medical professionals, most of them neurologists, who strongly disagreed amongst themselves as to whether he had Parkinson's at all (remembering that it is not something easily diagnosed.) He had the means to convene dozens of neurologists to examine him and try to reach a consensus. That was one thing he did.

But more than that, Brian wanted to look back at his life and see if there was anything that might account for Parkinson's. You will read about his twin grandsons, who were born with an exceedingly rare genetic condition, which means they will never be able to walk or talk or take care of themselves. This was a blow to their mother and father, of course, but it seems to have completely consumed Brian. He could not accept defeat: there had to be something he could do to cure these boys. Alas, there was not, and his beloved daughter came to the conclusion that she did not need to change her children; she could love them as they were, just as deeply as any mother loves her children. Ondine loves them for who they are, not for who they might become. It is almost as if Brian had to become these children, and then go through the process that his daughter did and learn to love himself for who he is. I am not sure he has succeeded as well as Ondine has, but by the end of the book, I had the feeling that he was on his way there. Brian seems to have stopped fighting. Ten years of fighting for the twins, and then another ten years of fighting for himself (the twins are now fifteen years old), seems to have brought him to a point of wisdom. I think.

Brian has never pretended that he has 'overcome' Parkinson's. I don't believe anyone has (though there are always accounts of miracle cures, and quite frankly, I don't believe them). I believe that Brian has done something even more important: he has retained the essence of his 'self'.

Nothing essential in Brian has changed. I mean that in the sense that his essence, who Brian is, the deepest core of his personality, has remained not just intact, it shines. Everyone who meets Brian today finds something mysteriously poignant and attractive about him. There is a kindness in his eyes – true, it has always been there, but now it is even more visible. When I meet him these days, I often find myself in tears – to which Brian, being Brian, responds with similar tears. They are not marks of sadness; I am not sure what they are. It is almost as if I am looking into his body and I see his soul, or whatever that something is that we recognise (when we are able to see it) as the innermost being of a person. Brian has always had this in him, it is just more visible today. Maybe that core is simply love. That's what it feels like to me.

'I Am and Always Be Brian Sherman':
Self Portrait of Brian with Miracle (2020)

Miracle at Home (2020)

Contents

Introduction	xv
The Biggest Battle	1
2010	7
2011	23
2012	37
2013	51
2014–2015	67
2016	79
2017	93
2018	105
2019	119
2020	139
A Medical Perspective Dr Stephen Tisch, Neurologist	155
Walking Through Honey – The Video Series Rod Freedman	171
Artworks and Photography	177
Acknowledgements	181
About the Author	183

'Hen': A Diptych (2021)

Introduction

It's morning and the night has passed. Inch by inch, centimetre by centimetre, my life force, my self, is being eroded and then, presto, the heavy veil covering my face slowly lifts. I know that I am slowly disappearing. The Brian Sherman you all once knew will be no more.

This cry from the heart was written some three years ago. It is the aftermath of a nightmare, literally and figuratively, and a low point in my battle with Parkinson's disease, which has now extended over ten or more years. Remarkably for a progressive illness, I have improved, but the war goes on.

I can't say exactly how it began. It's not one of those clear-cut things, where you feel unwell, notice a lump or some other symptom, go to hospital for a scan and receive a definitive diagnosis. This condition – my companion, my shadow, the self I have become – crept up on me in subtle ways, masking itself under various guises, psychological and physical. It took its time, revealing itself slowly and in fits and starts.

It inhabits me now. My days and nights are shaped by my invisible adversary, which fills my life with its presence. It is all consuming. It is what nightmares are made of.

In my search for a diagnosis and treatment, I have left no stone unturned. The road I have been on, and continue to walk, is long, winding – looping back and forth – and challenging.

PD can be perplexing. Its manifestations may vary widely from individual to individual. Then there is 'Parkinsonism' and a number of Parkinsonian 'syndromes' that share some of the symptoms, such as tremor and rigidity. Further complicating things, not everyone with Parkinson's, myself included, has the classic tremor as a predominant symptom.

The holy grail of a test to settle the diagnosis – a brain scan or pathology test, for example – is yet to be found. Misdiagnosis or late diagnosis is common. It is only possible to confirm with certainty via a postmortem, by observing the substantia nigra – the 'black substance'. This region, located deep in the brain, contains neurons that produce dopamine. In people with PD, the substantia nigra is depleted, and along with it, the dopamine that controls movement. I have read that by the time PD is recognised, the dopamine level in those affected has diminished by some 70–80 per cent. The disease, by some estimates, is thought to afflict some two or three per cent of the population and many millions of people worldwide.

Another aspect of my symptoms confounds the situation. Depression and anxiety, which I suffer, go hand in hand with PD. But these can also create PD-like symptoms in those who are free of the disorder. It's a case of chicken and egg, and that perennial puzzle remains unsolved.

Adding to the complication, the course of the condition is variable and can be very different from person to person. While the destination is known, the precise details of the journey there, and its duration, are not.

This project, documenting my life with Parkinson's, gives some comfort or solace. It will be a permanent record that bears witness to my experience. The story is one I feel somehow compelled to tell. It's a very human thing to want to share. I feel it is my civic duty to be open about my experience with this difficult journey in the hope that it may assist others with theirs. While the news from the frontline is not good, perhaps, it may create a sense of community with other sufferers. It might also give medical professionals an insight into the day to day lived experience of what it is to grapple with Parkinson's, at least from my own personal perspective.

My account of PD follows on from my memoir, mapping out in much closer detail how I came to be where I am with my Parkinson's, and tracing the ebb and flow of my days as I live them.

INTRODUCTION

Like my experience, what I present here is somewhat fragmentary, a dossier of observations that I hope will build a collective picture of my life with PD. I have reconstructed as best I can my symptoms, how they appeared, and the long quest for diagnosis and treatment. During the process of writing, I have kept a diary of my days, which forms a running thread in this work, bringing the story into the present. Thoughts from family form a key part of the book, and their reflections appear at the end of each chapter. I think there is a value in openness, in showing frankly the impact of this disease on those close to me.

I reflect, too, on whether there is an emotional dimension to my physical malaise, and the fact that I now have this disorder. We all know that the body and mind are connected. Did, perhaps, my past, and elements of grief and trauma in distant and more recent years, play a part in my PD?

My story is not one of redemption and deliverance from the all-encompassing clutches of my illness. It cannot be – unless there is some sudden miraculous breakthrough in treatment, which, to my knowledge, is not imminent. Clinical trials of various medical, pharmaceutical and surgical treatments are ongoing, but there is no cure on the horizon, as far as I know.

In the end, we each bear our battles alone, and this one does not end in victory.

Despite it all, I am aware of my great good fortune in life. I acknowledge I have the resources to temper the ravages of PD. And the fact remains that I am surrounded by love, from my close family and friends.

* * *

Throughout, my life my family has been my ballast. The long hours I put in when establishing and running EquitiLink did not detract from my devotion to them. I ensured my heart remained at home, keeping in touch daily with Gene, Emile and Ondine during my years on the road for my work. Family is, and always has been, the foundation of everything.

My mother Minnie moved to Australia and lived with us in Sydney until the children were grown, and she enjoyed an active social life well into her seventies. She passed away in her nineties, having been diagnosed with dementia some years before, much loved and sorely missed.

Gene's father, Eric, also emigrated, coming to Australia in 1980 to be closer to us in his later years as his health deteriorated.

Eric's life had been marked by great personal tragedies. His only son Peter's schizophrenia culminated in his untimely death from an overdose of prescription medication – accidental or not, we do not know. This followed Eric's years of fruitless and heartbreaking attempts to find an effective treatment for Peter. Eric's health was less than robust, worn down by the toll of caring for a son who could not be saved. He had already lost his wife, Mickey, to suicide, and, later, his assets were greatly reduced when his business partner swindled him.

There was another huge blow when he was diagnosed with Parkinson's. By the time Eric arrived in Sydney he was frail, his vigour and vitality exhausted, a shadow of the dynamic, highly successful Type-A businessman who had once been something of a role model to me.

There was little to redeem Eric's plight. He went into a gradual but steady decline as his infirmity increased. He compared the effects of his illness with the overwhelming sensation of being submerged in a jar of honey. The viscous environment suffocated him. There was no way out of the jar, it was impossible to dilute the contents, and the lid could not be opened. Movement was painstaking, slow and heavy, the tiniest incremental half-step required him to push with all his might against an invisible and always-present resistance; a force that, in the end, couldn't be overcome.

We attended closely to Eric's needs through all the years of his declining health. He passed away at the too-young age of 66, a day after Emile's bar mitzvah.

Now, with my own struggle with Parkinson's, I think of Eric's description of his experience with the disease. His words resonate with me and so I have called this book, *Walking Through Honey*.

* * *

I imagine my grandchildren reading this account of my later life, perhaps decades from now, as they are in middle age or older age themselves. It will likely be a time when degenerative diseases are a thing of the long-gone past, like some medieval scourge that modern science has banished to the history books.

Through it, they will come to know the reality of their grandfather's experience, for better or for worse. I can't be anything but authentic. I offer them, and my other readers, my truth. There are moments of light, but the cold, hard reality prevails. This is the way it is, for me, to have Parkinson's in the early 21st Century.

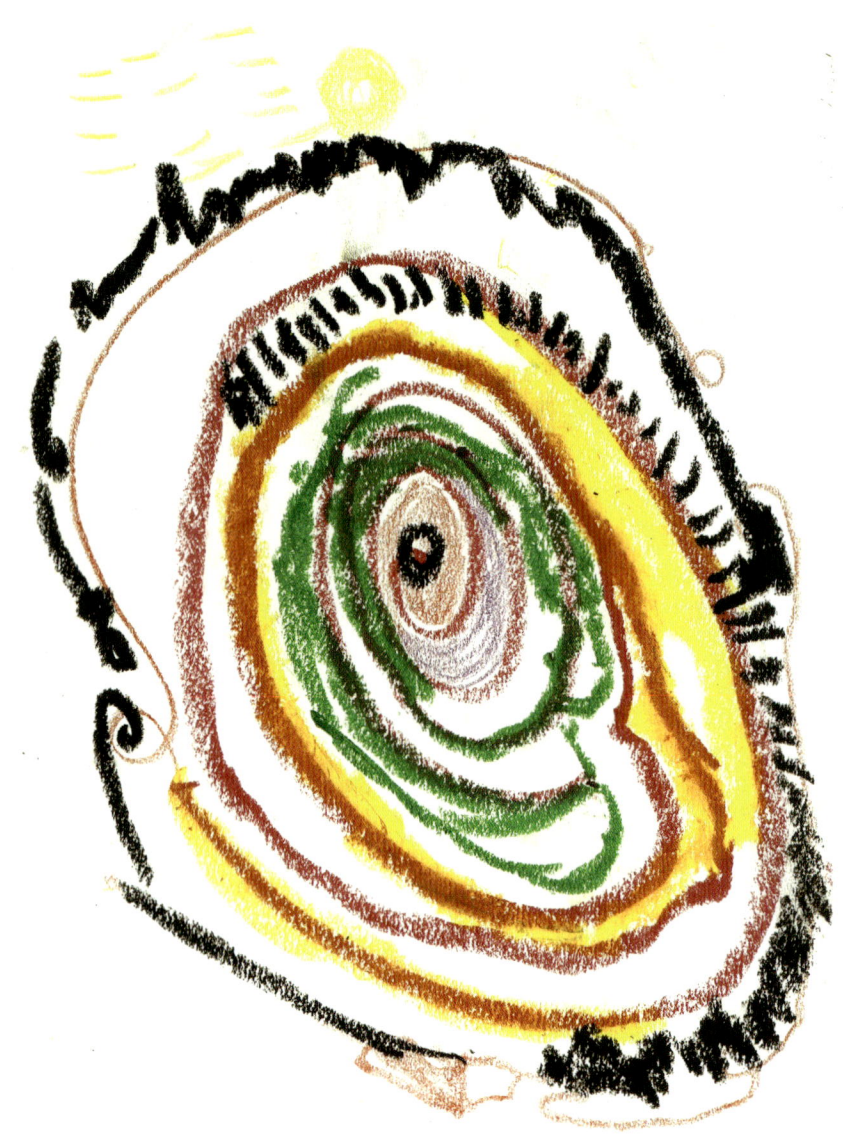

Heart of the Sea Urchin (2021)

The Biggest Battle

MONDAY, 4 MAY 2020

It's 1:20pm on a sunny autumn day in Sydney. I am at home, locked in due to COVID for a few weeks now.

I am feeling heavy as I do every day, locked in both by my body and by the situation. I take my 1:30pm pills and gag on some of them, as I do every day.

Too many pills.

COVID restrictions lifted a bit this last Friday. Gene and I went to Emile and Carrie's for dinner on Friday night. It was good to see them all and get out of the house.

Sunday we had friends over for lunch, keeping our social distance. It was really nice to see people and connect.

It's hard for me to participate in conversations but I do my best. Mind and body are not in sync. The body doesn't do what I wish, although in my head I know what I want to say and do. Frustration builds.

I often find I stutter and cannot get the words out. I know what I want to say but it takes a while to verbalise, and when I do, it's not always clear and people struggle to understand me.

During this lock-in period, Gene and I have watched movies every night for the past few weeks. This is the time when I feel calmer than usual. Movies and TV help me escape my reality, and I'm able to get lost in the story. I go to bed at around 10:45 each night.

The mornings are the hardest. It takes me some time to get moving. This morning I swam, even though it's getting colder outside and the pool water temperature is falling. Having my daily swim does refresh me somewhat. The cold water shocks the body. My love of cold water stems from my youth, where cold showers were the norm. I still only have cold showers to this day.

My afternoons are fairly busy with Zoom calls, such as my drumming lessons, speech therapy, physiotherapy sessions, Voiceless catch-up calls and other work-related Zoom meetings.

My yoga breathing teacher comes to the house, as does my massage therapist, even in these times. In between that, Natalie and I go through my emails, responding to those that demand a response, and we work on this PD project.

I play some table tennis each day, which I enjoy. I still have a knack for the game. Believe it or not, my reflexes are still pretty good.

A Heavy Heart, Being Lightened with Sunshine, Birds and Forest Green (2020)

Heavy Heart Carrying the Weight of a Whale! (2020)

'Have a Nice Day!': Message Communicated
with Identified Images of Tortoises Making
their Way Across the Page (2020)

2010

Where did it all begin?

To my recall – as imperfect as it is – the first solid intimations that there may be something not quite right with my physical health came around 2010, though even earlier there were inklings.

It's a warm afternoon in spring in the northern Indian state of Rajasthan. I am on a ten-day cycling trip with my daughter, Ondine, and son-in-law, Dror. We weave through rural villages, see women in brightly coloured sarees going about their work, their children at their sides, and take in the stunning desert vistas that typify the region. It is a welcome respite from the earlier part of our trip, which had begun in Delhi. There, I had witnessed the dire poverty that besets so many, the broken-down infrastructure, the noise, the sheer pressure of the masses, the cacophony of animals and vehicles, the crush of endless activity. Later, in Jaipur and Jodhpur we will enjoy the architectural beauty of the colonial palaces for which the regions are famed.

Throughout my business career in finance, cycling had been my go-to recreation. It is a departure from the cares and woes of fund management, the perfect opportunity to immerse myself deeply in the day to day lives of other cultures and step off the professional highwire.

I enjoyed numerous such trips, often with Ondine and like-minded adventurers, from the early 1990s onwards, and took them on with all my vitality. Italy, France, Ireland, Alaska, China, Cuba and Israel were among the places I rode, each for around seven days, in the company of friends, family – often Ondine and Dror – and tour groups, all of us eager for a down-to-earth, street-level experience of the textures and flavours of life in foreign lands. I was generally strong, fit and able, and confident in my riding, and I took enormous pleasure in it.

This time, however, I am not myself. For months before the trip I was uneasy. Somehow I don't feel right. I am unsure if I am up to the task of a demanding ride. Thinking back to the trip I took in Cuba some six years earlier with my brother Ron and his wife Mary, I recall that I had inexplicably overheated, and found myself taxed beyond expectations. Dror and Ondine, always with my best interests in mind, had encouraged me to commit to the India trip despite my protestations. They believed the adventure would do me the world of good.

It had been a harrowing three or four years prior to departure, and the thinking was that cycling would be a tonic. Now, hovering tentatively on the saddle of my teetering bike, I wonder if I still have it in me.

* * *

In 2006, Ondine and Dror are living in Israel. They welcome much wanted identical twin boys, Dov and Lev, in December, brothers to their daughter Jasmine, born in 2004. As with all births, the boys' arrival is met with great rejoicing by the entire family.

The twins come home and at first all seems well. But before too long, there are signs that things are not quite as would be expected. After a few months, Dov and Lev still do not smile or make eye contact. Their neck muscles are not able to support their heads. Developmental milestones are missed. As the months go by, things do not improve. The boys are unable to roll over or hold their bottles. They do not make the vocalisations that babies typically do.

From the time of Ondine and Dror's earliest suspicions, there begins an odyssey in search of a diagnosis. It will continue until 2008, stretching the family to the limit.

Dror and Ondine, with Gene's and my support, embark on interminable rounds of consultations with various specialists – paediatricians, developmental neurologists, endocrinologists and more, some ten or fifteen in total. The boys endure every test, screening and examination under the sun. We are determined to identify the problem: diagnosis is necessary for us to provide Dov and Lev the best possible treatment in the timeliest possible way.

However, to the family's dismay, little light is shed. We are told they have 'dystonia' – abnormal muscle movements including both reduced muscle tone and some heightened tone, or spasticity. Prognoses vary wildly from the encouraging – 'They will come right' or 'They are slightly delayed, but it is benign variation from the norm' – to the devastating – 'The boys will never walk and never talk', the latter delivered by a senior specialist with a stunning absence of empathy. A specific diagnosis, however, eludes the pantheon of medicos.

To say it is a testing time is the understatement of the century. I know that, as the boys' loving and utterly devoted parents, Ondine and Dror bear the brunt of the situation. However, I find myself overwhelmed. I develop anxiety, which builds to fever pitch, and I am often beyond exhausted. I feel I am carrying within myself a heavy weight.

As Ondine focuses her boundless energies and love on the boys' and Jasmine's wellbeing, Dror and I go into overdrive, seeking answers to the conundrum of the twins' condition. Hour after hour, day after day, our time is devoted to this quest. We partner up to contact eminent physicians and researchers around the world, sending them dossiers on the twins or visiting in person, pushing and pushing beyond endurance. Each lead is a dead end. It cuts to the quick every time.

I decide to get in touch with the business contacts I have built up over many years to leverage their connections with senior medical specialists who may be able to help. One is a well-connected CEO in the US who has links to a major children's hospital. He puts us in touch with a clinician with world-leading expertise in neurogenetic disorders of childhood.

After some negotiation, this doctor is persuaded to look into our case. Amongst possible diagnoses he includes the rare X-chromosome linked genetic condition, MCT8 Deficiency (Monocarboxylate Transporter 8), also known as Allan-Herndon-Dudley Syndrome (AHDS).

The disorder, which mostly affects boys, involves a mutation in the genetic coding that deprives the brain of the thyroid hormone, T3. Without it, the normal formation and growth of nerve cells in the brain, as well as the development of junctions between nerve cells where cell-to-cell communication occurs, cannot take place. Severe and lifelong impairment of physical and cognitive abilities is the result. The disorder is exceedingly rare, with, at that time, some 50 families in the world impacted.

After several weeks of ratcheting apprehension, the answer we fought for with every fibre of our beings is in. But it is not as we had hoped. To our utter shock, the tests are positive. Dov and Lev have MCT8. The family is reeling. Gene suffers a debilitating bout of depression. As for me, a kernel of grief, profound and long lasting, is planted.

* * *

By the time of diagnosis, it is 2008. Over the succeeding years, Dror and I again go into battle, scouring the far reaches of the globe for an effective treatment or cure.

I fund research, and I convene conferences with Dror bringing the best medical minds to the task, with the assistance of a paediatric endocrinologist with world-leading expertise in thyroid related diseases. We have meetings once a year, inviting some 30 clinicians and researchers from around the world, to brainstorm the latest research and opportunities for treatment.

I make an elaborate high-stakes arrangement involving international deals and much intrigue (all legal) to purchase a supply of a medication that is near impossible to obtain. According to a paediatric endocrinology professor who heads a prestigious research centre in Germany, this is the one drug that may have some positive effect on the boys' conditions.

After scrupulous weighing of the risks and benefits, and utmost due diligence with respect to treatment clinics, the boys also undergo therapy with stem cells, and later, two more rounds.

Our hopes are not to be realised. There is no miracle, in the traditional sense. My determination to surmount any challenge – a deeply rooted tenacity – has stood me in good stead through my entire business career. Yet this quality is powerless in the face of MCT8.

Dov and Lev's condition is not able to be mitigated to any great degree. The boys do not walk. They do not talk. They cannot turn over unaided. They likely never will.

However, they are well, happy and enjoy life to the fullest each and every day. Their abilities far exceed their dire prognoses in many ways. They have the most wonderful parents in Ondine and Dror and sister in Jasmine. And they are loved and cherished just as they are. The idealised version of normality I had so desperately sought for them is unattainable, and it is my challenge to understand that that is okay.

I know this, and I feel in my heart, mind and bones that I have done all that can be done. Nevertheless, something inside me darkens precipitously.

* * *

In India on our ride in 2010, I sense that I am falling down, metaphorically and literally. Somewhat dizzy and increasingly queasy, I have developed a fear of getting on the bike. My capacity to exert myself is generally diminished and I am much slower than on my previous trips. I lag behind the other riders, and on one occasion I got into the support van, which is unusual for me; previously I would lead from the front, thanks in part to my competitive streak. For some time now I have been taking antidepressant medications, and I am not as social as I used to be. I feel a shift at a fundamental level; a sense that all is not well with me.

Over time, though, as we ride further, my vitality builds and I feel that I am regaining lost ground. There is an uptick in my mood and physical capacities. Towards the end of the trip, I come off my medications. It is an error of judgement. On my return to Sydney I hit the doldrums with a vengeance.

THURSDAY, 7 MAY 2020

2:15pm

Had a fractured night. Felt I was awake for most of the night.

Woke this morning, the usual stuff…stretches and so on.
No swim, it's too cold. Had breakfast and read the papers, as I do every day. I notice this is an improvement from, say, six months ago when it was a battle for me to read. I could not seem to focus on the words in front of me.

I am dealing with the knowledge that this is a degenerative disease, yet how can I be better than six months ago? I can't help thinking maybe it is not actually Parkinson's. Is this just wishful thinking? Perhaps.

Natalie is here every afternoon and we work on these PD diaries. It is very helpful as it clarifies some of my confusion.

This afternoon I have a massage at the house, which eases some of my tight muscles. The body seizes up somewhat with PD, and for me, no amount of stretching can totally undo the tightness.

We are then chatting to Dror via Facetime, as it's his fiftieth birthday today. I miss Dror and the family very much. It will be good to connect.

I try to hold on to the positives, yet every morning I feel that I don't know how I am going to continue.

MONDAY, 11 MAY 2020

It's 1pm

Saturday I was not in a good state. I can't really remember much about why I felt so 'off'. We had people at our house for dinner. It is an effort, no matter who it is. Fatigue is one of my greatest enemies.

Gene went to the hairdresser but I did not have the energy to go. I am tired most of the time.

Right now I'm seized up all over. My face feels as if it's also tight. If I were to look in the mirror, would I see a scrunched-up face?

It takes every ounce of energy to keep my eyes open. When I am tired, my legs seem to give way and my movements become jerky. Is this the dyskinesia getting worse? It is hard to discern what is what.

I have a session with my therapist today at 2pm. I thought I was physically going to her office but, of course, we are not – not yet anyway, due to COVID. Feeling a bit confused. Have occasionally been unsure as to the date and what day it is, especially at the moment given the lockdown. Every day seems the same.

Another thing is puzzling me. As I look at an insect or any object in my vicinity, it seems to change form in front of my eyes. I can see a leaf and know it's a leaf, yet after contemplating it for a while, it seems to alter its shape. Very odd. Perhaps it's my vision changing.

Brian Sherman's movement therapy (Brian cycling on a stationary bike), multiple exposure composite photograph by Gary Grealy

Gene

Brian went on dozens of cycling trips with Ondine and Dror, and with his cousin Lloyd, but he never, ever got into the vehicle that follows the riders in case anyone gets into trouble. When I heard that he kept getting into that backup car, I thought, My God. Prior to their trip, he would rather have died than give up. So I knew that something was just not right.

Also, at that time he was still messing around independently (not under medical supervision) with his medication. 'I'll take this. I won't take that. Add a little bit of this…' This has been Brian's lifelong modus operandi in relation to his own health. He never had serious health problems before PD. However, whenever he did have health issues, and when the nearest person gave him advice, he tended to follow it – forging his own path, independant of medical advice. I remember Ondine saying, 'Dad's just given up this and taken on that.'

This pattern started years ago. When he went on the roadshows in the EquitiLink days, he used to take a whole stash of medication; he often took antibiotics then stopped taking them. He decided, no, this lot wasn't working, and he tried another tactic.

Ondine

As that bicycle trip to India got closer, Dad started panicking about it. There was a lot of anxiety. He was really suffering already in the lead-up to that trip. Dror and I didn't really understand why he was so panicked. We felt a little bit like, 'What? Get your act together… don't overreact. It's going to be fine. You know, if you need help along the way, you can always get into the van and we're going to be there.' It's a totally supported trip and he's done so many challenging bike trips in the past. Then it became clearer and clearer leading up to it that he was not feeling confident. And when we went on the trip, he just wasn't himself at all. I mean, he was really at the back.

He is a very competitive guy. Always on our biking or hiking trips, he was very aware of where he was in relation to everyone else and would be beating everybody and not wanting to ever, God forbid, get into the van. I would occasionally get into it when I just couldn't be bothered fighting anymore. So for Dad, getting in the van was like the worst possible thing one could do.

I really felt for him because he was kind of trailing behind and needed the support of staff. There were always two people riding with us from the company, one in the front and one in the back to make sure that everybody was safe and accounted for.

I guess that was the first time I really got a shock that things were not good. But then again, leading up to that point he had been on medication for depression and anxiety. On that trip, being out and exercising all day, even though it was challenging, he felt a rush of endorphins, and decided to take himself off his medication without any consultation or discussion. At the time I thought, Okay, well, if he's feeling much better, maybe this is what he needed. But when we got back to Sydney, he totally crashed and went into a bad kind of funk. And I think really after that trip, the serious symptoms started.

He'd cry, you know, he'd be in tears all the time, and just not able to smile. I'm trying to think of the moment when Emile won the Oscar. We had an event to watch the Oscars live and I remember us saying at the time, 'Wow, it's the first time he's smiled in a long time.'

Dror

Before we went to India, we went on a trip to Los Angeles to meet a senior doctor We were trying to rope him in to do research on the boys' condition, MCT8, and to get his feedback on doing stem-cell therapy, which we wanted to do in Panama. We were going to Panama after LA.

We were in a hotel that was about two kilometres from the hospital. And I noticed that while we were walking back to the hotel from the meeting, Brian was dragging his leg and not walking properly. Brian likes to walk, so that was one of the first signs for me something was going on. A much earlier sign came way back in 2004, when we went for ride in Cuba with Lloyd, his cousin.

Cuba is hot and humid, and Brian had real difficulty handling it, beyond the normal, beyond everybody else, really. He was very sensitive to the heat, which he hadn't been in the past. I noticed that he wasn't handling it very well. I didn't know to put it down to Parkinson's or anything in particular. Now, when I look back, I'm sure that was probably the first sign. And it repeated itself on subsequent training rides that we did in Sydney, in preparation for other bike rides. There was a ride that Brian did later, in South Africa with his brother, Ronald, where he just couldn't handle the ride.

It wasn't about the heat at that point. It was about maintaining balance and Brian feeling unsteady. This was really unusual because Brian's a massively experienced bicycle rider. These were the tell-tale signs. After that experience in LA and then seeing Brian continue to shuffle in Sydney, we started to discuss what all that meant and what was going on with him. Maybe he was having some kind of nerve issue, or maybe he was stressed and perhaps traumatised and that's why he responded this way. We were looking to do more exercise to shake him out of it and we then went on that bicycle ride to India. I think that was the beginning of Parkinson's.

Abstract Freedom with Dominant Black (2021)

*The Appearance of an Image of a Lion:
Representative of the Strength of Dealing with
the Difficulty of Shallow Breathing* (2020)

Fragments of Time (2020)

2011

Back home in 2011, I am feeling quite unwell. There is a deep sense that I am not my usual self. My formerly plentiful energy seems to have deserted me, and I find myself flagging more and more as time goes by. I begin to experience a range of symptoms, or at least sensations in my body that are unfamiliar to me. They start in my right leg. Somehow, my leg feels as if it is rubbery, instead of solid bone and flesh. I feel that it is not within my control. Walking is more of an effort, slower than my former pace and with a slight shuffle of the feet. Nor am I as mentally fit as I had been. A fuzziness creeps in.

By this time, I have a growing sense that there is something at play. Ever the entrepreneur in pursuit of my next project, I take to googling my symptoms with a building sense of purpose and urgency. After the difficulties of the preceding years, I wonder if my general malaise is trauma-induced rather than the effect of some insidious disease. Still, on the basis of my research, I suspect a physical dimension to my symptoms. After much research, I come down on the side of Parkinson's. I decide to consult a well-respected Sydney neurologist with expertise in the disorder.

It is a landmark moment – the first step on my journey into the netherworld of PD.

It's 9.15am on a bright autumn day. All looks right with the world, but in my heart of hearts I am expecting the worst. I enter the consulting room of the doctor's small suite. It does not help that in the waiting room I see patients clearly in the throes of their own difficult journeys with neurological illness. The ghosts of my future? I turn to contemplate the mature tree swaying in the breeze outside the window.

It is the first time I will undergo a full neurological examination. The specialist has a professorial demeanour and is thorough and accommodating of my questions. He has me move my arms up and down, tests the pressure of my ability to push and grip, has me walk a line, follow a pen with my eyes and touch my nose, and he taps my joints to check reflexes. And so on and so on. I can see he is making sure that every base is covered. He also records a detailed medical history. I had brought along with me the results of various tests and scans gathered over the preceding months for him to review.

I wonder if this is it.

The truth is, for some time I had had my suspicions about Parkinson's. I can't help but think of Eric, immersed in his metaphorical jar of honey, enfeebled, the simplest movement excruciatingly arduous as his PD took hold.

The news for me, however, is good, and the neurologist's conclusion clear.

I have examined Brian...in detail and I think that there is some very, very mild slowing on the left side, and he is aware of this as well. However, I do not think it is enough for me to say...that he has Parkinson's disease. I am looking very hard for something...

Some months later I again visit, and the doctor reaffirms his position:

I can't find anything today that would make me feel that Brian has Parkinson's disease. He walks perfectly well; he swings his arms perfectly well. He has a mobile face; he is not particularly stooped. Pushing it as hard as I can, he may have some very mild rigidity... on the left side, but there is no bradykinesia [slowness of movement] and there is no tremor.

Anyone else might breathe a hallelujah at the news. But perhaps due to my natural inclination to test boundaries, I am not convinced. I believe further investigation is needed to understand what is ailing me.

As it happens, I continue to consult this conscientious and dedicated specialist throughout my journey, and he continues to maintain that the diagnosis is not PD. At one point he says to me in frustration, 'Brian, repeat after me: *I do not have Parkinson's.*'

I have no real reason to question his professional judgement. Parkinson's is an enigmatic beast, and I did not and do not show the typical symptoms of tremor and so on. I wonder if the humanity in him made him less inclined to affix me prematurely with a damning label that there is no escaping.

* * *

It does not help that at this time I am having increasing trouble with my eyes. Over a period of years my vision has been worsening due to the slow but persistent growth of cataracts. I have surgery on my right eye, followed by the other a few months later. I am worried and I have good reason to be. The procedure is an unmitigated mess, exacerbating my growing giddiness and nausea, and failing to correct my vision. In fact, it makes things considerably worse.

The first surgery does not go well, as the ophthalmologist who operated acknowledges:

Brian had routine right [cataract] surgery on the 3rd of February 2011. Unfortunately, this was complicated by postoperative cystoid macular oedema which needed an intravitreal...injection. Following this, the macula returned to normal and has remained that way, and he now has 6/6 unaided vision in the right eye.

In layperson's terms, the retina became swollen postoperatively. When cortisone drops fail to settle the issue, the next treatment for this complication is reminiscent of medieval torture: an 'intravitreal' injection of cortisone directly into the eyeball. If I was trepidatious before, my anxiety is now off the charts.

I'm taken into the procedure room and asked to recline on an examination bed. Next, eye drops – anaesthetic, I assume – are given. The specialist inserts a set of metallic spreaders into my eye, wedged under the top and bottom lids to separate them and hold them open. It is a deeply unpleasant sensation having any foreign object in the eye, but this surely takes the cake. I am told to direct my gaze away from the surgeon's hands, which loom beside me with the syringe, toward my other eye. He punctures the surface of my eye and pushes the needle into the white. I feel more pressure as the cortisone is injected. I can say categorically that I have no wish to endure a needle to the eyeball ever again.

With vision restored to normal limits in my left eye, the plan is to operate on the right eye to make it shortsighted. In theory, the two would then work together to produce what is called monovision, allowing clear sight at any distance.

> *I went ahead with surgery to Brian's left eye on the 10th of November. It went well and there were no macular problems. I aimed to make the left eye myopic to give Brian monovision, with the aim to make him as independent of glasses as possible for all his normal day to day activities as well as public speaking. Unfortunately, in his case the monovision has not been successful. His optometrist has been able to help with glasses for near, intermediate and distance.*

Rather than monovision, I am delivered a visual soup. Focusing on the near, the intermediate and the far is impossible. I feel the world is swimming before my eyes.

I use the prescribed glasses for near, middle-distance and long-distance vision, but it is unwieldy as I awkwardly try to manage switching between them. I am given soft contact lenses. I spend a long time struggling to place them in my eyes, and they induce a severe anxiety reaction in me. I am unable to tolerate them. Next, it is prism glasses, intended to correct the double vision the surgery has left me with, but they are useless.

Admittedly, I had been experiencing melancholy before this sequence of events. Having said that, I wonder to this day whether the imbalance in my eyes after this surgical road-to-nowhere has had an impact on my neurological and emotional condition.

When I am reviewed by this doctor the following year, the situation has moved on. I have sought further medical opinions on the question of PD. He makes the following observation, which carries worrying portents: *'No doubt the lack of success with monovision is contributed to by possible early Parkinson's as well as anxiety and depression.'*

* * *

Around 2011, I start to consult with a psychotherapist. I find the sessions beneficial and arrange several appointments per week. The analyst has some enlightening perspectives to offer and poses questions that I find useful to ask myself.

Prior to seeing the analyst, I had had long and mixed experiences with a variety of mental health professionals. From about 2007, I consult a psychiatrist about my increasing psychological distress and melancholy. She and I have a good relationship. This doctor feels I am suffering 'acute sadness'. I certainly can't deny that is the case. Whether the insight is illuminating is another question. She tries me on a variety of medications, but nothing provides any kind of remission of my unease.

There follows a psychiatrist who is overly partial to pills. I am prescribed a potpourri of antidepressant medications, flipping from one combination to the next with no relief. Each time, I endure symptoms of withdrawal. Finally, he tries me on lithium combined with Nardil, an older antidepressant that is also meant to reduce anxiety. The combination produces serious vertigo. It is altogether a disaster.

Next, I see the head of a leading psychiatric clinic at a major hospital. I undergo an elaborate formal assessment of my mental state, involving multiple tests and taking several hours. As part of the process, I complete a lengthy computer-based questionnaire and am grilled on my medical history, past episodes of depression and social history. The psychiatrist concludes:

Brian has developed symptoms of clinical depression and has been treated appropriately with a variety of antidepressants. Though these have offered some benefit, none has led to recovery or even sustained remission. Remarkably Brian continues to 'soldier on' and in addition to the many efforts that he has initiated as regards helping his grandchildren, he continues his many other roles, financial and philanthropic.

Interestingly, he has thought that his psychomotor slowing may be because of incipient Parkinson's disease and though he has seen a specialist and been reassured countless times he raised this with me as well. However, even a brief albeit non-expert examination reveals that he does not have an intention tremor, the classic gait, Parkinsonian like [facial expression], and though it is difficult to categorically state that he will not get Parkinson's disease, at present there is not sufficient indication that he has anything other than the psychomotor changes associated with severe depression.

So, his diagnosis is in. He finds only psychomotor changes – also known as psychomotor retardation or PMR – the slowing of physical actions and flattening of cognitive abilities that can accompany severe depression.

Again, one might think I would be relieved. Still, I have my doubts.

Finally, after seeing two other therapists, I connect with the psychotherapist whom I see to this day. I discuss with her my foreboding sense that I may have Parkinson's – though, of course, I acknowledge I am completely unqualified to judge, would not wish the diagnosis on anyone, and have been reassured throughout by my first neurologist. We dissect in detail my daily mental struggles, my various physical symptoms and my increasing anxiety and feeling of general unwellness. In her view, my problem is part depression, mostly anxiety, and she concurs with the psychiatrist that PD is unlikely. She feels firmly that my psychological and emotional state is generating the symptoms I am experiencing, such as weakness in my legs.

THURSDAY, 14 MAY 2020

To bed very late last night, around 1:30am. I went to visit Zachy to help him with his school project and I stayed there until about 9pm. Emile brought me home. Watched TV with Gene, then looked at the Sherman Family Board meeting papers. Eager to get it all in my head before today's meeting.

Woke up feeling very heavy and tired, not having had my usual hours of sleep. My hip was painful this morning, but I'm not feeling comfortable to go back to physio due to COVID. Possibly in two weeks' time.

It's a wet, rainy day and my mood is low, possibly due to my weariness. Who knows these days?

Every other day I have my blood pressure taken. In PD, blood pressure fluctuations are a serious issue. I tend to have low blood pressure generally. Sometimes it falls to the extent that I feel nauseous, weak and unable to support my body.

On the other hand, there have also been times when my BP has been elevated – so high that on one occasion the top figure, the systolic, reached close to 210 and I ended up in the emergency room. I discovered that I was taking too much of one particular medication. I immediately reduced that pill to once per day and, thus far, it's been better, albeit today rather high at 179/97 (sitting).

I believe that everyone who has PD struggles to varying degrees with their blood pressure. Getting the balance is no easy feat. For no apparent reason, it can jump, and equally plummet. The wild swings are unsettling; another thing to contend with.

* * *

Ondine and my brother Ron's daughter, Danya, and I take a short holiday at the end of 2011, at Canyon Ranch resort in Arizona, where Gene and I had enjoyed many restorative breaks over the years. It is great to spend time with them, but by now, the activities that are meant to replenish and invigorate – such as biking and hiking – have lost their shine for me. I feel weak and tired, my bones and muscles tight and stiffer than I recall feeling before. I reduce my riding level of difficulty to half of my previous status. During the one hike I have with Danya and Ondine, I set a snail's pace. I feel low, and much of my time on the holiday is spent consulting doctors. There is a battery of tests, but nothing much comes of it.

With a group including Ron and Mary, I bike South Africa's Cape Peninsula for eight days. Dramatically changed since Apartheid ceased, it nevertheless conjures so many memories of my childhood and earlier adult life – the sights, smells and sounds; spectacular nature all around.

We ride to an outdoor tavern that Ron and I had visited a number of times during school holidays, which our uncle managed for many years. On a day trip we take in the idyllic white sands of Muizenberg Beach, where we swam so many decades ago as kids.

It should have been a wonderful respite from my woes. However, inside me, something is giving way.

The eight days of biking are difficult. I ride less than half of the time, and there isn't much muscle behind my efforts. Downhill, I am afraid on steep inclines. I have to push myself to ride at all. Even when not on the bike I feel woozy and unsteady.

Quite often, I leave dinner before anyone else. I don't feel like socialising. One evening, we all go to the movies in Cape Town. I feel a little better during the film, but I revert to dizziness afterwards. My lightheadedness reduces when sitting or lying down, watching TV or reading, but resumes in other circumstances.

My walking is still slow, too slow for my age, and there is rigidity in my posture.

In terms of my emotional state, I am unsteady. When I talk on the phone to my family I begin sobbing and am unable to speak. My propensity to break down is now much more acute.

Of importance, I can't face going to Brakpan, Johannesburg and a family dinner with Ron and Mary. Ron is exceptionally keen to share a brotherly trip to our youth. I just can't do it.

MONDAY, 18 MAY 2020

1:26pm

It's groundhog day. My mornings are still very rough. It's cold and damp out there. When I woke up I felt awful, but a little better now.

I am constantly aware of the short period of time I have left on earth. When I launched my memoir two years ago I didn't think I would make it, yet here I am, complaining as usual.

We had people over yesterday for lunch. It was okay. Yet it doesn't matter where I go, where I retreat to, I cannot get away from myself. There's no respite, or not much. I am able to lose myself a little, but only for short periods when I am distracted; for example, in a board meeting, watching a movie, having lunch with family and friends.

Family remains everything to me. Last night Gene and I went to Emile and Carrie's place for dinner. I gave the kids a hug for the first time since COVID hit. It felt so good.

My journey through this disease is not simply physical. Equally devastating is the mental health dimension, specifically anxiety and depression.

For a long time, I had the sensation that I was jumping out of my skin due to anxiety. This has diminished somewhat, but perhaps the depression is now greater. I feel locked in by my body. It's hard to convey how this affects me on an emotional and psychological level.

On top of this, my movements are laboured. I am better sitting than walking around. I used to love walking, but I struggle with it now.

We moved to Lang Road for a few reasons, one of which was to be close to the wonderful Centennial Park and yet, now, I don't go there much at all. Even visiting the park is a considerable effort. I will try to make the effort to do so, as I simply must. I cannot stop, cannot fade away, frozen. I must get up. I must.

Emile

I think the journey of Dad's ill-health has been very bound up with the emotional journey that started with trying to find the diagnosis for Dov and Lev. It was a sort of breakdown that seemed at the time to encompass both emotions and a physical decline.

We all thought that it was emotionally driven. There was a whole range of emotions at play that couldn't be explained by a disease like Parkinson's. But at the same time, Dad felt it was more than just emotional, that there were genuine physical things happening, and so he was on a quest to work out what it could be.

The first key thing that I remember was his eyesight [around 2011]. He had eye surgery, and your eyes are meant to adjust very quickly. He was in a quite emotional state at that time, but his eyes just didn't seem to adjust well, or he was anxious about it and didn't believe they did. And he went to an optometrist, 30 times, 40 times; he got five different pairs of glasses to try to correct the problem. And he felt dizzy all the time. We really thought it was anxiety, and an emotional collapse that seemed to be precipitated by his obsession with diagnosing and curing Dov and Lev.

But for me, that emotional collapse had been brewing for many years after he'd sold EquitiLink and started to become fixated on a whole lot of really dark issues. He became increasingly anxious and depressed. This moment felt like a natural tipping point. Dov and Lev were not the sole reason, but they became the catalyst. And within all of that, there seemed to be physical manifestations.

Dad was always convinced that it was more than just a psychosomatic reflection of what was happening emotionally.

He would go and see a doctor after doctor, and it got more and more intense. People would say, 'It's definitely not Parkinson's' and 'We don't know what it is.' But I think if I trace it back and look at the physiological Parkinson's link, I go back to that moment with his eyesight, which seemed to show that the muscles in his eyes were not adapting as quickly as they should have done under normal circumstances.

Mood Changes I: 'Joy in Colour' (2021)

Activity (2021)

Yellow Mustard in a Sea of Blue (2021)

2012

My situation does not improve when I return home from South Africa. There is little or no relief from my symptoms. I feel weaker, more anxious, and generally unwell. Is my condition psychological or physical? The question runs around and around in my mind, a continuous loop that I struggle to shake. I decide to seek further medical assistance. I see a senior professor of psychiatry at a mental health institute.

It is a sign of how difficult my suite of complaints is to diagnose that he cannot be confident as to what it is that is ailing me. He notes cogwheeling in my arms, a jerking movement when the arm is rotated; this is a characteristic feature of PD. He cannot, however, exclude depression as the basis for my motor and psychological symptoms.

Brian is concerned he might be developing Parkinson's disease and has seen a neurologist on a couple of occasions and been given an 80 per cent assurance that he does not. The possibilities are that he is experiencing a melancholic depression in line with the characteristic psychomotor disturbance that he is showing. However, there is no family history and, as I did note some cogwheeling, I think the differential diagnosis [the process of differentiating between conditions with similar symptoms to settle on a diagnosis] needs to be broad.

I ask if he thinks I may be mimicking, in some subliminal way, the experience of my father-in-law, Eric, as he battled PD – the exhaustion, increasing rigidity and general difficulty in movement. He doesn't feel this is the case. The professor says he has had some success in treating melancholic depression with Ritalin, the drug they give to hyperactive kids, and decides to start me on it. While initially there seems to be some improvement, the effects, I feel, are too strong, and despite careful adjustment of the dosage I decide over time to come off it.

On my return for review, there is something of an ominous shift.

This is a follow-up to my initial letter. I reviewed Brian last week... and also had the opportunity to go through all the medical material that he had accrued during his assessment in the United States [at Canyon Ranch]. At the end of that assessment, I favoured a pseudo-melancholic picture rather than seeing melancholia as the primary diagnosis. In considering the former, I would favour the likelihood of Parkinson's disease and have since made contact with Brian's neurologist.

He orders an MRI, but it reveals nothing of note.

For me, it's back around the carousel again. I return to my first neurologist. My malaise is deepening, and I still seek clarity of diagnosis. He reaffirms his opinion – I do not, in his view, have PD.

MARCH 2012

I have taken six different antidepressant pills over five years to no positive avail except, probably, a reduction of anxiety. Have had some bad side-effects.

Is it my eyes, my anxiety or fear, or PD that is causing many of these symptoms? Weak legs, dizziness, nausea, lack of usual enthusiasm...

Am I suffering from sadness, depression and anxiety due to the genetic condition of Dov and Lev and my obsession with finding a cure? I self-diagnose Parkinson's disease via Google and, again, become completely preoccupied. Am I suffering from Obsessive Compulsive Disorder?

I become confused as to emotional and physical issues.

I consult with a number of therapists and psychiatrists over a nine or ten-year period.

Eventually, I'm not able to discern what is causing this giddiness, this nausea.

I think I can rule out depression. I don't seem to have the normal symptoms of depression…What is it then?

* * *

As 2012 continues, my symptoms are unabated; in fact, they continue to mount. I am generally slow in my movements – the medical term is bradykinesia. My voice has dropped in volume, sometimes almost to a whisper, and I have difficulty modulating it – this is known as hypophonia. I am less expressive facially, which my family has noticed. My right leg continues to feel rubbery, as if it could give way at any time. I am constantly fatigued. Dizziness continues to plague me, including a sensation like rocking on a boat, and there's a lag in vision. In terms of triggers, head movement, bright lights and stress set me off. Emotionally I am on a short fuse, with my tendency to sob still in full force. I feel spaced out, not altogether in touch with what is going on around me.

Professionally and socially, I start to struggle a little. Meetings, speeches and surmounting reams of paperwork become difficult. In social situations I am easily tired out. Standing for long periods and engaging in animated conversation test my limits.

I have a strange encounter with a psychologist who specialises in Cognitive behavioral therapy. I explain to him the continuous vortex of dizziness I find myself in, accompanied by the feeling I am about to faint and fall. His response is novel. He tells me I should just allow myself to faint and fall. He has me sit in a rotating office chair and swings me around and around. The idea, I suppose, is for me to confront my fears, and through exposure, to become desensitised to what I am afraid of – hitting the ground in a dizzy spell. He suggests I sit in a small, heated room to get over my sense of things closing in on me –

precisely by creating a situation in which things *are* closing in on me. Our therapeutic relationship does not last long.

Ondine and Dror suggest that I speak with a young neurologist friend of theirs. He has offices close by, and Ondine accompanies me.

In retrospect, it is a diagnostic turning point. May 2012 is the first time a neurologist will put a diagnostic label to my condition, albeit with what at first seems like some equivocation. After thorough examination and history taking, the neurologist's opinion is that I have 'an element' of PD. I am not clear on what exactly this means. I write to him to seek enlightenment:

Brian: *Your report says I have an 'element' of PD. Can I have the symptoms I have but not have PD – i.e., can one be a little bit pregnant, i.e., have a little PD?*

Doctor: *I suspect this is early PD, but you do have slowness of movement, that makes you pregnant (not a little bit pregnant). There are other conditions that can mimic this, but I feel your clinical picture is consistent with early PD.*

Brian: *And finally, is it possible that I am mimicking PD symptoms given the severe traumatic emotional state I have been in and closeness to my father-in-law who had PD?*

Doctor: *I have seen this but very rarely. It is very hard to do (subconsciously of course) but the cogwheeling I feel is a little too hard to mimic, even subconsciously. So no, I don't think so.*

It is all exceptionally confusing. His senior neurological colleague – the very first specialist I had seen, in 2011 – continues to categorically exclude Parkinson's. It's a split decision between the experts, with no resolution in sight.

What am I to make of this? I am in a kind of limbo, suspended between the differing convictions of the specialists. The older doctor's adamant stand against diagnosis is a beacon of hope, which, of course, springs eternal. Yet my concerns remain, and there is one clear benefit of a definitive diagnosis: treatment can begin. I worry that indecision will delay action on therapy that could reduce the symptoms and, I hope, manage the progression of the disease, if it is indeed PD. On the other hand, I worry – even more so – that if it is PD, the walls are really closing in. I have visions of Eric, incapacitated, straining to walk, and trapped in the jar of honey.

MONDAY, 25 MAY 2020

3:35pm

Feeling better than I was earlier today. I came into the office at 12:30pm but after around half an hour my vision blurred. Natalie said I went very pale and was cold and clammy, always the signs of low blood pressure. Immediately, I lay down on the floor with a book under my head and my feet up on a chair for around twenty minutes. I began to feel better and the colour came back to my face. I stayed in the office for around an hour. It was good to be back there, even though there are only three people present due to COVID.

    Gene and I watched a movie on TV last night. No matter how hard I try, I cannot find the movie in my mind, nor the title. I find it distressing that I cannot remember; it shows that my short-term memory is shot to hell.

    About to have my session with Tomer: drumming.

    The weather is windy and cold, and there is no better place to be than at home.

* * *

The young doctor suggests I have my ears tested in the neurophysiology department of a nearby hospital. This will help determine if an issue with my middle ear may be causing my nausea, and the unsettling sensation of being off kilter. Warm water is flushed into my ear canals. I get the all-clear.

He proposes a trial of a drug called levodopa. Developed more than 50 years ago, it remains the cornerstone of treatment for Parkinson's to this day. It is a precursor to dopamine, the neurotransmitter that is reduced in people with PD. Levodopa converts to dopamine in the body, to help control the motor symptoms of the disease and normalise movement. I am keen to try it, as it might just shed the light I am seeking. If my symptoms fail to respond to levodopa, it is taken as an indication that PD is not present.

I start the drug in 2012 and remain on it for several months. The dosage is adjusted in increments to ensure that I am receiving the optimal amount. I persist, even as my symptoms show no signs of remission. In the end, there has been no benefit. The likelihood, then, is that I have dodged the PD bullet. As good as this outcome may seem, my condition belies it. I remain in the dark as to the cause of my dilapidation.

It's time to up the ante. On the recommendation of my first neurologist, I consult a neurology professor in a southern capital, an expert in movement disorders.

We arrange for me to fly there. I make a mental note as to my PD scorecard: my original neurologist maintains I do not have PD; one professor of psychiatry thinks I have PD; one thinks I do not; the second neurologist thinks I have early PD; the failure of levodopa indicates it is probably not. I am giddy just thinking about it.

The doctor is efficient and thorough in his examination. I've done this dance before – walking up and down, arms rotated, finger to nose, arms outstretched, shoulders shrugged, tap me on the knees – and on and on and on. He gives little away during the consult. But in the end his assessment is clear.

I think the motor signs are neurological in origin and not the result of psychomotor retardation as part of a depressive illness… [However], there are no specific clinical or radiological signs to focus a differential diagnosis. The lack of response to levodopa makes Parkinson's most unlikely.

I update my tally. Original specialist: 'Brian, you do not have PD'; professors of psychiatry: one PD, one not PD; second neurologist: PD; third neurologist: not PD.

What then is ailing me? Back to square one.

* * *

Later in 2012, I take a walk around our neighbourhood in Woollahra, as I have done many times over many years. The weather is fine and mild, and I feel like I am making reasonable progress given the decline already evident in my stamina. Admittedly, I tend to shuffle now, and my pace has slowed, but this is a fairly good day, relatively speaking. Approaching me is a specialist who lives nearby. We say hello and exchange a few words whenever we cross paths. As usual, he stops to have a quick chat. He asks if I have Parkinson's. A few weeks later, there is another encounter with a senior doctor in the neighbourhood. As with his colleague, we are friendly and greet each other if we happen to meet on the street. When he too asks if I have PD, it is beyond coincidence. What am I to think?

Matters are not helped when I notice, at this time, a serious deterioration in my handwriting. Always small and somewhat difficult to decipher, it is even smaller now, and becoming cramped, as if I am running out of space on the page. I struggle, too, with typing into the tiny keyboard of my phone. Yet, I tell myself, I have been assured time and again it is not PD, and the weight of senior medical opinion, and my lack of response to levodopa, continues to put me on the side of the negative.

Perhaps more worryingly, there is a tremor, albeit very slight, in my right hand. I see it as a possible harbinger of doom.

FRIDAY, 29 MAY 2020

1:30pm

Had my first pills around 8am. Am awake, but just to take the pills, so not all together 'there'. I fall back to sleep and wake again around 10am. Thankfully, I can get out of bed myself. I do some stretches and then get into the shower. We have a photo shoot this afternoon for the *Australian Financial Review*, so I went to the hair place to get tidied up.

There is quite a marked difference between my days and nights. At night, generally speaking, I feel more awake, more alive. The 'veil' lifts a bit and I seem to feel more connected.

Right now, though, my face is taut, like a facelift without the benefits. My breathing feels somehow controlled; it does not flow freely. It's as if I cannot ever take in enough air to breathe.

Gene

There was a long period when we didn't know what the matter was.

When first he got into the backup wagon on the cycling trip, well, that didn't mean he had Parkinson's. No, it could have meant a thousand other things. Then he reported a band around his eyes, his head, which sounded like a migraine of some kind. So, that didn't say Parkinson's. Then he had an eye issue, and the doctor, without asking for permission or telling us, adjusted his sight for long-sighted vision, and there was a whole story around that.

There were a thousand symptoms, such as rubbery legs and tightness around the forehead. His first neurologist said, 'He doesn't have Parkinson's. He hasn't got it. I've seen the disease so many times. I know what it looks like.'

As for acceptance, I don't know. I don't think we've had a full coming to terms, but I do think we've moved in the direction of reluctant acknowledgment.

We're lucky we have all the ingredients that mitigate a tragedy in that we are blessed with a loving family, and have supportive and loving children. Ondine calls every third or fourth night. Dror calls at least once a week. Brian still sees Emile at the office, and we see Emile and Caroline's children every weekend. We are so fortunate that Emile married Caroline. Her family is enormously compatible with ours in terms of family values.

One of the key props when you face a really bad situation is clearly a loving, supportive family. They have been an enormous help and a real blessing. On the professional side, we've found a brilliant therapist. We came to her at the beginning of our journey with the twins, and for me she was a saviour. After the twins were diagnosed, I had a nine-month nervous breakdown.

Brian and I see her together weekly and, in addition, Brian sees her individually. These professional sessions significantly cover the emotional side.

Our house, has been created for Brian. We bought it because of him. We restored the building to its historic self, adding modern day conveniences. It was renovated, refurbished and put together with Brian's interests first and foremost.

He has, for example, some special requirements in the bathroom. I briefed the interior architect in great detail. No fittings should look like they would in a hospital. Everything is going to be custom made, which we've done. There is a seat in the shower so he can sit down. It looks like a piece of sculpture. Every aspect of the house is aesthetically beautiful – even the bathroom.

The entire house is on one level, there is not one single step, small or large.

Something that Brian can't access but doesn't need to, is a little studio apartment built on top of what were the stables. We use it when we have family and artists as guests.

The garden is not big, but it's big enough for our purposes.

So instead of Brian going out to people – he has difficulty getting in and out of cars – people are coming here.

I think all of that has supported Brian emotionally. Exactly as I had hoped.

Abstract Mark-Making:...Identified Dog Image Adding Joy to Otherwise Difficult Day (2020)

Waking Up (2021)

'Watching in Colour': Emotional Release (2021)

2013

In 2013, my quest continues. I am evaluated by a range of experts, in endocrinology, immunology and integrative medicine; the latter takes a more holistic approach to disease and focuses on alternative treatments.

The endocrinologist finds I have osteoporosis, for which I begin medication. I also have pre-diabetes. He places me on a drug to treat blood sugar levels, and to prevent my condition escalating to diabetes type 2. I am hopeful when I read that this treatment is speculated to have benefits in PD, and there are potential trials relating to its ability to slow or stop the disease's progression. The re-purposing of existing drugs that have undergone testing, where the safety of the drug has been established, is a fertile area. It offers the prospect of bringing new PD therapies into use more quickly than with novel medications.

Every day, I have to inject the drug into the subcutaneous tissue on my stomach. I find the process emotionally difficult but persist for many months. Unfortunately, there is no appreciable effect.

At this time, I also have scans, imaging studies and tests, none of them enlightening to any notable extent.

I begin to see another psychiatrist. He tries me on various medications, but whatever is afflicting me – psychological or otherwise – is refractory. Of increasing concern is the number of drugs I am taking or have been on. Sedatives, antidepressants, cognitive enhancers, stimulants, small doses of antipsychotics used for anxiety and depression, and the diabetes and osteoporosis meds, to name only a few, and, once more, levodopa. I try it again, to discern if there is any benefit. If it alleviates my symptoms, this would be suggestive of a PD diagnosis and give me the certainty I somehow, perhaps perversely, crave. It doesn't.

It can't be to my advantage that my system is dealing with multiple medications. One drug might have a certain effect, but in combination a variety of medications may create unexpected side effects with unanticipated consequences. Since each person is different, with a unique set of genes and individual metabolism, a medication might work for one person but be totally useless or adverse for another. In any case, the potent mixture of chemicals circulating in my bloodstream must confound a clear analysis of my condition.

I feel stuck. I'm unable to disentangle the multiple threads – what part is physical illness, what part is my mental state, and what are the side effects of my meds?

I am fearful of changes in treatment that could be to the detriment of my vulnerable state. But I also cannot help myself, always seeking the next medication or consult.

It is not helpful, I come to think, that Western medicine separates the body into systems, with doctors developing super specialisations in one or the other part and treating only *that* system with medications, surgical procedures, and so on. It is as if the mind, the province of psychiatrists, is distinct from the mechanics of the body, and the brain, the remit of the neurologists and other physicians. The overview of the whole person is lost, especially the subtle but powerful interaction between the psychological and the physical. And a bath of pharmaceuticals is added on top.

Later that year, I travel to Israel. Ondine and Dror, Jasmine, Dov and Lev had moved there in late 2012, after four years in Sydney. It was a blow to lose them, but I perfectly understand Dror's powerful need to be in Israel, and Ondine's to make a happy home with their family. We have kept in close and constant touch, including visiting in 2012, and the bonds remain as strong as ever. Our mutual love and affection are undiminished by great distance. I watch from afar as Jasmine blossoms, and the boys, with all the love and care in the world, continue to enjoy life and make strides. The move has been a good one for all of them, and to my great delight, the family is doing well.

On arrival, I am struggling. I feel exhausted, and my anxiety is unabated. There remains some weakness in my left leg, and my formerly purposeful stride has now definitively slowed. I am less able to lift my feet. Some tremors continue in the right hand.

While in Israel, it is my intention to do further investigation to unravel my medical mystery. Dror has arranged for me to see two top specialists in neurology. One is amongst the ten or twenty most highly regarded internationally, and works with the Michael J Fox Foundation, an organisation that leads the world in funding groundbreaking Parkinson's research. Within a short time, they both assess me.

After the usual examination, the eminent physician notes cogwheeling of both arms, rigidity, slow short, shuffling steps and decreased arm swing, as well as hypophonia, the low voice typical of Parkinson's or related syndromes. He concludes that I have 'Parkinsonism' at '2.5 H&Y'.

I look up the reference. The Hoehn & Yahr scale assesses severity of symptoms. Zero signifies absence of Parkinson's-like symptoms and 5, the most advanced state. My rating of 2.5 denotes mild symptoms on both sides of the body. It indicates that I was able to recover from the 'pull' test, where the doctor stood behind me and pulled me backwards, challenging me to maintain balance. In the physician's view, my neurodegenerative condition is of a slowly progressing nature. This medico also makes a note that I am suffering from depression.

The other specialist is prepared to call it: *'My diagnosis would be of idiopathic Parkinson's disease of mild-moderate severity. Briefly, I do not find good evidence for any other Parkinsonian syndrome.'*

Both suggest I go back on levodopa, which I do. One emphasises that intensive physical exercise, physio and hydrotherapy will be key to staving off the ravages of PD.

* * *

I had long been interested in the potential therapeutic benefits of stem cells. Some years earlier two of my dogs, beloved companions who had had pain in their lower spines and difficulty walking in older age, had been treated in the hope of improving their mobility. The results were outstanding. Stem cell infusions had restored their ability to run, to play as they had done years earlier, and to bound up the stairs like younger versions of themselves. While researching possible treatments for Dov and Lev in the years after their diagnosis, Dror and I had also attended a conference in San Francisco with 500 leading stem cell experts, and I had been impressed by the potential advances on this new frontier.

Nevertheless, I well understand that stem cell treatment is essentially experimental, in humans and in animals, and outcomes are not guaranteed. Israel happens to be a key centre for stem cell research and clinical applications. After much due diligence and consideration, we had organised for the twins, Dov and Lev, to have treatment at a leading clinic there. There were no ill effects, although equally no clear and unequivocal evidence of benefits. I begin to seriously consider it as part of my own treatment options.

While, to my knowledge, stem cell treatment as a therapy for PD is in its infancy, I believe there has been some promising research on benefits for neurological disorders. One thing I do know is that the current treatments for Parkinson's are severely limited in scope, treating only the symptoms. The hope with stem cells is that they may go to the root cause – the depletion of dopamine producing neurons in the brain.

I have always been inclined to take calculated risks, and this, to my mind, is no different. I decide to investigate the therapy at the Israeli clinic that treated Dov and Lev. We know it is reputable and its facilities and medical staff are first class.

Prior to treatment, I am given a full assessment. The clinical director writes:

General impression was that of Parkinsonian appearance with a low soft monotonic voice with abnormal gait consisting of small steps and instability. General physical examination was unremarkable...No major loss of muscle strength was observed and hand and knee reflexes were normal...normal finger–nose test with slight intentional tremor and shaking hands...Writing capacity using his right hand and ability to draw requested objects was somewhat disturbed. No sensory loss was noted.

The general impression based on the above and considering reports of prior imaging suggested either an ill-defined neurodegenerative disorder or what seemed to us to be more likely Parkinson's disease.

He confirms that the proposed stem cell treatment has the potential to improve signs and symptoms of neurodegenerative illness. Further, he says, it is safe, based on more than eight years of experience in more than 250 patients. My hopes rise when he assures me that his clinic's documentation suggests that stem cells can repair damaged neurons, as well differentiate between neural stem cells and 'dopaminergic' neurons – those responsible for producing the neurotransmitter dopamine.

My mind is made up to go ahead.

The treatment is administered via lumbar puncture and an intravenous drip. Under light sedation, I am placed on my side on a surgical table, with my back near the edge. I'm required to bend into a foetal position to separate my vertebrae and enable the needle to be inserted into my back. The infusion of stems cells derived from cord blood runs over twenty minutes or so. I must lie flat for some four hours afterwards to prevent possible complications.

The injection is followed by a procedure to help improve blood flow to the brain and shunt the cells to the appropriate region – the substantia nigra, home of the dopamine producing neurons. I am put into a frightening looking machine that encases my head like a mechanical shroud. It emits low-energy acoustic shockwaves that, I am told, promote take-up of the stem cells in my central nervous system.

As the contraption does its work, it pushes my anxiety into overdrive. Despite the sedation, I am completely alert. Immobilised, trapped and panicking, I envision a future in which I am helpless and vulnerable, a prisoner in my own body. Anxiety I am familiar with; it is my constant companion. But this takes my panic to a new level. I become severely distressed at the thought that this is a foretaste of what is to come for me. The stem cell treatment itself was straightforward, but the addition of this element makes for a traumatic experience. On top of it, I am left with a shocking headache; a feeling of intense pressure in my skull.

Nevertheless, increasingly desperate for any measure that will improve my state, I determine that I will try the treatment one more time. Turns out I am too optimistic.

On this occasion, the doctor decides that to improve my chances I should have three exposures with acoustic shockwaves prior to cell infusion and three exposures post infusion. It is not to be. *'Unfortunately, patient developed an anxiety state and we could not complete the treatment as planned.'*

The session is aborted. Still, I return for a final time, and have one more treatment with cells derived from placenta and cord blood, and one session of acoustic waves.

Perhaps the sedation has been increased. I manage to cope and am hopeful that I will see benefits in due course, ideally sooner rather than later. Yet, to my great disappointment, there is no appreciable effect. It is the end of my adventure with stem cells.

On my return home to Sydney, I am not in a good state. I am told that I am barely functioning, almost comatose, my eyes glassy and my demeanor deadened and inert. My family and colleagues are worried for me. On my journey with Parkinson's, it is a low point.

Post my visit to Israel, my son Emile takes the situation in hand. He writes to the family on the state of play and next steps:

Hi All,

This is the summary of the plan of action we discussed.

Brian has been diagnosed with Parkinson's or Parkinsonism. Essentially, a neurological condition that the top neurologists say is Parkinson's or Parkinson's related.

We all know that Parkinson's is a clinical diagnosis, and it comes in many different forms with different symptoms. The treatments are personalised, but the drug levodopa is the key starting point to treat it.

Plan of action

Now it's clear that there's a core neurological condition, Dad needs to be overseen by a neurologist and not a psychiatrist. In fact, one of the drugs he's been taking until recently (the antipsychotic) is known to negate the effect of levodopa. Dad has been misdiagnosed for a long time now, by [his original neurologist] and others, with the flow-on effect that he's been misdiagnosed by the psychiatrist, who says he's got obsessive compulsive disorder as he's so obsessed with Parkinson's, when in fact he does have Parkinson's!

Dad has come off the antipsychotics of his own accord, and wants to come off the anti-depressants. It feels like the right thing to do. We need to treat Parkinson's now, and have the neurologist oversee his condition. He's been on antidepressants for 6+ years, partly to deal with his stress over a physical deterioration that everyone thought was in his head.

I want to go to the psychiatrist with Dad as well, and he should come off antidepressants under supervision.

We can look at the anti-anxiety medication (and the uppers that he takes to combat the effect of the anti-anxiety meds) in the next stage. But I think Dad really wants to now come off these pills and focus on the Parkinson's. We're all concerned that the various pills and their side effects are clouding the issues, as well as Dad.

New Neurologist

[The original neurologist] has misdiagnosed Dad for so long, and he's made other errors such as getting Dad to do a PET scan rather than a DAT scan. The Israeli neurologist said a PET scan is useless and he needs to do the DAT scan to see what's going on with the Parkinson's. The neurologist's other error is having put Dad on levodopa, knowing that he was also on antipsychotics. Levodopa apparently doesn't work if you're on that drug.

We all want Dad to now be overseen by a top neurologist who we're totally confident in. I'm researching the right person... It's the neurologist who now needs to oversee his condition, including all drugs he's taking and the interaction of drugs.

Physical Side

The most important treatment for Parkinson's (aside from the right drug) is to do strong physical exercise which stimulates the brain. Dad hasn't been doing this. It's not just going on the walking machine himself. We agreed that we'd find a hydrotherapist as well as a personal trailer/physiotherapist so that he has a session each day at 10am for an hour of proper therapy. This is absolutely key.

Nutrition

And of course, it's key that his nutrition is good...I personally want to look at the full range of pills he's taking, as we all think it'd be good for him to reduce pills and take a more healthy food and lifestyle approach.

Other Medical Tests

There are two medical tests that have been recommended as important. One is the DAT scan, which he should do asap. The second is the lumbar puncture to check auto-immune condition but this should only happen two months after the DAT scan, as the stem cell treatment he's just had will distort the lumbar puncture test now.

Think that's it!

Let me know if we're all on the same page. We love you, Dad.

Emile

Meanwhile, my original specialist adheres to his original view – that I do not have PD.

TUESDAY, 16 JUNE 2020

2:20pm

Lovely winter day – sun is shining. Busy house with lots of workmen around doing this and that. Right now I am feeling okay. Had that hip/lower back pain when I woke up, but it seems to have settled.

Had a relatively good day yesterday, which feels unusual these days. More often than not, my days/nights feel like a struggle. No real understanding why yesterday was a better day.

Had an appointment via Zoom with my psychiatrist. In order to prescribe another drug for memory loss, he needed to do a cognition test on me. For example, What is today?, Where do I live?, Who is the PM? I was also required to count backwards from 100 in 7s. The doctor laughed at just how well I performed. I did this test in 2019 and he said I had done a better job this time. There is also a drawing component. I had to copy a relatively simple diagram, two boxes intersecting. I managed quite well. Could not get it 100 per cent right but mostly. Not sure if I will go onto this new drug; I will discuss further with the neurologist next Monday.

The night before last I woke up around six times, and I had taken a sleeping pill! Had a better night last night.

Last week was hard. My lower legs and feet are tight and swollen. At one point, the GP thought I may have a DVT and sent me for an ultrasound in both legs. Luckily, I am all clear. It's hard to know why swelling has become an issue; I guess it's part of PD and also perhaps a side effect of some of my meds. I am now wearing compression socks each day, I need to keep my feet up when I am sitting and walk as much as possible to maintain the blood flow. Also drink lots of water.

Found a new physio. She will come to the house every week.

My dreams have started up again. Last night's was puzzling: In the dream, I am in the forest with three other guys, locked in a hut. Someone with a large knife wants to get in and kill us. There is a conflict between myself and the other guys. I am more of a commentator than a participant. The situation is unresolved. When I wake up, it feels real.

Brian Sherman's movement and speech therapy (Brian completing a circuit of neck and shoulder muscles stretching), multiple exposure composite photograph by Gary Grealy

Carrie

We had all travelled together to South Africa to celebrate Gene's seventieth birthday. Ondine, Dror and Jasmine from Israel, all of us from Australia. We were staying in a beautiful game reserve, sitting around the lunch table overlooking the bush, in such a perfect spot. Brian was unable to catch his breath. He was so anxious and depressed, and there was great uncertainty as to what was wrong. He struggled to pull himself out of the debilitating anxiety, and seemed to feel hopeless and helpless.

Brian has always felt like the even keel of the family, and it seemed now that all his energy was being taken up with sorrow and sadness.

I remember Emile sitting with him doing breathwork and relaxation. I think I recall Brian was trying different medications, and was confused as to what was going on.

Nevertheless, through all of that he managed to go out each day and be surrounded by nature and his family. He always responded well when he was with the children.

Gene

I am stronger than I thought I would be. I battled with depression, for nine months, before finally beginning to regain my equilibrium. I thought I'd be a wreck for the rest of my days.

I think Sherman Centre for Culture and Ideas (SCCI) has helped me in dealing with Brian's journey. I had created an original structure in my mind but also made it up a little as I went along, and now have to recalibrate (as does everyone) in the light of COVID requirements.

I am pleasantly surprised as to how strong I feel. I genuinely say, cross my heart and hope to die, that I have been truly blessed to find a man like Brian and to have had him by my side for 50 plus years. Very few partnerships are as happy as ours have been. I'm aware of this. I'm sure there are other such unions, I know of some, but also know that near perfect harmony between two people is not the norm. Divorces are common and many partnerships end in trauma. Everyone experiences loss during their life. Oftentimes marriages and partnerships can't take the pressure that comes with outside trauma.

Ours did. Ours was strengthened by the trauma which we had right from the start.

Our wedding had to be cancelled when I fell seriously ill. We originally planned for 150 guests. We wrote saying, 'Gene's very ill, there can be no wedding at present. We'll let you know as the situation unfolds.' We subsequently had a very small wedding with 26 guests, on 11 June 1968. Had we married as originally planned, I would have been 20. By June 1968, when we finally married, I was 21.

Looking back at my life, is really looking back at my life with Brian. My entire adult life has been spent with him. A long journey *à deux*.

My strength, I think, comes from two sources: one, the feeling of being blessed to have had Brian in his heyday, and the fact that he supported me through all my trauma. So I'm 100 per cent by his side now.

I am currently tidying up our affairs. Not our financial affairs, Emile's taken the reins there, but our art collection and the flow-on of our life together. The collection comprised 900 works which I plan to reduce to a core collection of approximately 300. I would like to have an exhibition at a major museum. We are selling 'capsule' collections via auction, and we have put in place a series of wonderful donations – gifts destined for the Art Gallery of New South Wales, the National Gallery of Australia, the University of Sydney's Chau Chak Wing Museum, the Art Gallery of South Australia and also the Lake Macquarie Regional Gallery. Emile has chosen the works he wants and is in the process of refining that. Ondine ditto.

Our family albums have been categorised, catalogued and uploaded into an online Dropbox. On the morbid side, we have acquired two grave sites, with markers for our parents and eventually for us. Buying plots for one's grave clearly signals preparation for the end…

'Softly, Softly', Reflecting on Feeling of Comfort
When Resting with Dog – Pepper (2021)

'Laying Around', Brian's Reflection on the Softness Felt
when Spending Quiet Time with Pepper (2021)

Freehand Abstract Colour Fill (2021)

2014–2015

In early 2014, I travel to Los Angeles. A senior medical contact who assisted with the twins' treatment has made me aware of an international expert in Parkinson's based there. He heads a highly reputable PD clinic that uses cutting-edge deep brain stimulation techniques for Parkinson's and offers DAT scans. I'm willing to try almost anything, within reason, to resolve my situation one way or another, and access appropriate treatment, as long as it is based on sound evidence. Dror, who has been so helpful in my dealings with the medical profession in Israel, and my brother Ron, attend with me.

Prior to our meeting, the physician has me undertake the DAT scan, a highly specialised imaging procedure intended to differentiate Parkinson's from other conditions that may mimic it. On the day, a radioactive agent is injected into my arm. It circulates through the body to the brain, depositing itself in molecules associated with dopamine neurons. A person with PD will typically show a lower concentration of the tracing agent in the relevant region of the brain. I sit for three or four hours while the substance does its work. Then I am placed on a table with my head strapped into a cradle to ensure I remain perfectly still. For some 30 minutes a scanner passes over my head.

I meet with the specialist and undergo the usual examination. I had gone back on levodopa since seeing the specialists in Israel, and it has begun to have some effect in moderating my symptoms. To my mind, this is mostly to do with helping me to feel slightly steadier and lessening my anxiety, rather than having any profound impact on my motor symptoms. I cannot say for certain if the change has been significant. I am now off the medication, to ensure my physical condition is not masked by the drug.

The clinician thinks my responsiveness to levodopa, albeit limited, potentially suggests PD. However, he is scathing of the DAT scan results. They show severe depletion of dopamine transporter molecules deep in my brain. He says this is entirely incompatible with my physical presentation and the clinical findings of his examination. These, he thinks, suggest only very mild, early stage Parkinson's. He rips up the test results before my eyes, saying the machine is a primitive device and the results often spurious, with false negative and false positives not uncommon. His words are reassuring: 'I do not treat images, I treat people. Brian, you do not have severe PD.'

In his view, I should be able to proceed with little escalation in impairment for years to come. Progression of symptoms is likely to be very slow. The rate of development, he says, is related to the time of onset. If you get PD early, it is likely to progress more rapidly, but that is not the case for me. He prescribes ongoing intensive exercise, one of the best ways to ward off further deterioration and stabilise the condition for as long as possible. As for deep brain stimulation, he does not think I am a candidate for it. He says it should not be considered for some eight to fifteen years down the track.

Meanwhile, back at home, my original specialist remains unconvinced that I have PD.

* * *

I continue to feel cactus. As the year progresses, there is no real change for the positive. My family – Gene, Emile and Carrie, Ondine and Dror – are there for me in every way, a constant reminder of my good fortune. Yet, my anxiety levels seem intractably stuck on 100 and my physical symptoms persist. There is the feeling that doctor-hopping and over-medication with multiple drugs – 'polypharmacy' – may be contributing to my situation. Clear sighted analysis of my condition is impossible and a path forward difficult to discern. In this respect, I am arguably my own worst enemy. I do ask for pills, and some doctors are only too willing to prescribe. I do seek multiple opinions, further muddying already murky waters.

In late 2013, Emile decided to take on board my medical maelstrom. Our close relationship has deepened even further over the years. He is now the adult child closest to home, so he is more involved in my situation on a daily basis. We share adjacent offices and interact often, both at work and in family time. He will continue to attend appointments with me, as his time allows, and track medical developments.

With the support of the family, he suggested I curtail some of my pharmaceutical use under medical supervision, which I do. I begin to focus more on the alternative means of regaining my health – or at least preventing further dilapidation – that the various doctors have prescribed. This includes, first and foremost, regular exercise, which I do with a personal trainer, and walking. I also take on hydrotherapy, yoga and light boxing training customised for PD.

Nevertheless, wherever I go, there I am. I am marooned in my body, which increasingly refuses to do as I say it should. Worse, my mind, which has been my strength and my core, has become an instrument of torture.

* * *

It's early 2015, and with the agreement of the family, I decide to seek a further opinion, to settle the matter once and for all – if that is indeed possible, given the lack of any definitive diagnostic test and the high potential for misdiagnosis, which is a feature of the illness. Still, I'll do whatever it takes to enable effective treatment of my symptoms.

I see a professor at a large teaching hospital in Sydney, a specialist in Parkinson's, on the say-so of my original neurologist. He leads a movement disorders clinic, so I will have the benefit of multiple minds focused on my case. He gives his patients as much time as they need, so appointments are delayed. After a three-hour wait, we are finally able to see him. I go through the standard neuro exam. He is particularly attentive to my history and current state, and I appreciate the close attention to detail. At first he's not convinced I have PD, but makes reference to dystonia. I note the parallels to Dov and Lev's initial diagnosis.

> *I can detect what I think is very subtle right leg dystonia on walking, as well as some dystonic movements of the neck mainly when performing fine motor movements…Therefore, I am not sure whether he has very mild Parkinson's disease manifest only as some leg dystonia and dyskinetic movements of the neck, with any other signs being masked by levodopa, an isolated dystonia syndrome, which could be either idiopathic, genetic or even drug induced. I agree entirely with [the specialist in Los Angeles] that the DAT scan findings are much more severe than would be compatible with his clinical findings even if he did have Parkinson's disease, and I therefore agree that it is most likely a spurious result. To try to clarify the diagnosis, I have recommended and he has agreed to review at our Combined Movement Disorder meeting.*

THURSDAY, 18 JUNE 2020

2pm, at the office

Last night, after a dinner at Emile/Carrie's, I had a fall! I was at the top of the stairs on the street level and lost my balance, propelling forward from the outward door onto the middle of the road. I could see the road coming towards my face. I must have put my hands out instinctively, which protected me. My knee and hands were bloody but luckily nothing was broken. Emile helped me up and I was able to walk to his car (he gave Gene and me a lift home). Gene and I were both a little shaken up. Got home and Kristina cleaned up the gravelly wound on my knee and I took a Nurofen.

Slept okay. Didn't take a sleeping pill. This morning I felt 'normal' – everyone was surprised at how well I have recovered from the fall, which could have ended badly.

Yesterday I was in the office with Natalie and started to feel very jittery and unwell. I had taken my Parkinson's med that contains levodopa a little late and I could really see the result of this. I was heading into an 'off' period. I took half a Serepax and two Nurofen as my right leg had seized up and felt so tight.

I had the sensation that I was jerking around a bit. It was awful.

Eventually it settled, and I felt a bit better. Oh, the perennial rollercoaster of this illness – a ride that I cannot get off.

* * *

Meanwhile, my appointment with a group of clinicians who specialise in movement disorders looms early in the year.

I duly turn up at the meeting, accompanied by Emile. Twenty or 30 specialists are seated before me in a horseshoe formation as I go through my paces. I'm an old hand at this now – the neuro exam. There are some questions and extensive discussion of my condition. The lead clinician videotapes my walk. I feel like a human specimen in an experiment of which I want no part. Nevertheless, it is necessary.

The verdict is stark, but I cannot claim it is surprising: *'At the Monday Movement Disorders meeting there was universal agreement that Mr Sherman has signs of mild Parkinson's Disease.'*

* * *

Despite my ongoing struggles, I am determined to come into the office every day. Many of my involvements continue and I am never not busy.

In my professional life, and increasingly in dealing with my medical condition and many appointments, I have my loyal Executive Assistant, Natalie, at my side for seventeen years. She provides exceptional logistical and moral support, underpinning my efforts to maintain both my health and my engagement in the world at large. Natalie works closely with a colleague, Ron, who takes over in the later afternoons, ferrying me to my various appointments and assisting me in myriad other ways. I am expertly supported in all my business dealings by long-standing legal counsel and director of the Sherman Group, Barry.

Alongside family, they are my core team, and I am grateful to have them.

My passion for animal protection is completely undiminished, and I work with Ondine in furthering Voiceless's mission to create a world in which animals are treated with respect and compassion. I continue to manage Aberdeen Leaders, later CLF, a listed investment company.

Throughout this time, I remain heavily involved with AIJAC, the Australia Israel Jewish Affairs Council, and continue as chair of the Rambam program, sending young leaders on fact finding missions to Israel. My philanthropic work through the Sherman Foundation continues, as we fund medical research, conservation, arts, animal rights, humanitarian and Israel related causes.

I don't have it in me to rest on my laurels, notwithstanding the difficulties I face with my physical and mental health.

Throughout this time, I am working on my memoir, *The Lives of Brian*, with my team: writer AM Jonson, Natalie, and Shelley contributing interviews with family and associates. It ends up being an epic tome of some 100,000 words, published by a leading university press – Melbourne University Publishing. The appearance of the book is a major high point and boosts my mood for some time. People are generous in their assessment, and there is a wonderful response from friends, colleagues and associates, and even from those I do not personally know. The book is favourably reviewed in a leading national newspaper and an extract is published in a popular weekend news magazine. From the vantage point of my current state, it is comforting to reflect on the full life that I have led.

FRIDAY, 19 JUNE 2020

1:35pm

Another beautiful winter's day. The sun is shining. Had physio and then speech therapy.

My whole body feels weak and tired but despite this, I managed my sessions as I always do.

Having vivid dreams, but cannot remember them at all, just the sense of an active narrative life at some deep level. Perhaps my psyche is working through the existential challenges I confront.

The weeks are just flying past. My days feel shorter as they really only begin at midday. This change in the sense of time is now part of my life, another side effect of my condition.

THURSDAY 25 JUNE 2020

Feeling okay; not great. My blood pressure is all over the place – a bit high right now. I think my body is adjusting to the new dose of meds, and it's to be expected.

It's a lovely day out there, but I feel I can't enjoy it. I used to love walking but now it's become so hard to go out and walk for the sheer sake of it. We will see how it goes. I now use a walking stick most of the time, even at home. It helps steady me, offsetting the forward propulsion motion.

Had a vivid dream last night. In a hospital bed, my breathing had become more and more laboured, leading to ultimate death. It seemed very real. When I woke this morning and got out of bed, it was dispelled. I wasn't fighting the dream; it felt very natural and peaceful. Family were visiting.

I have my personal trainer at 2.30pm. I do squats and stationary biking. My legs were always so strong but are no longer. I am trying to regain some muscle tone and strength.

On Tuesday night I went to Emile and Carrie's for dinner as I usually do. I was much more careful going up the stairs when I left. No fall this time!

I enjoy spending time with the boys. We play table tennis and I look over their homework with them. Cy plays the trumpet (actually, not sure which instrument…could it be the saxophone?). He played together with Emile – a duet, which is lovely to see.

Dror

I think Brian is in much better shape emotionally now – in the last two years – probably than he was in the four years preceding the diagnosis.

He was just going through the degradation of his physical facilities, fighting it, trying to do whatever he could to push through. Not that he's not suffering now, but he was suffering immensely also on a psychological and emotional level.

Depression. Anxiety. Taking a lot of pills to curb his anxiety that were also bringing him down further. I mean, he was taking enough pills to tranquilise elephants, a testament to the emotional despair that he was in. I can only imagine what it feels like to see your physical abilities just slipping away every day, bit by bit. And he was having symptoms, some of which he has treated now, but that were really debilitating; dizzy spells, feeling the world swirling around him. He carried that for years until he realised he was suffering from loss of blood pressure.

He couldn't move at certain times of day. He wasn't very particular about when he took his medication, and timing is everything, so he couldn't function. I think this was in part because there was a lack of acceptance of the condition, and also dealing with it wasn't head on. He probably lost about two years of knowing that it was Parkinson's and not taking the medication, or, often, not at the right time.

For ages, Brian and those of us in his support team were kind of fumbling around, and not being very precise.

I think that in the last two and a half years or so, Brian has come to accept that he has Parkinson's; and not only him, but his family and the people supporting him: Gene or Emile, Ondine and me, or his brother. Then as he himself and those around him have accepted that he has Parkinson's, his treatment of the condition has become more precise. And although it's very sad and I wish he didn't have Parkinson's, he's actually been better since his condition was diagnosed.

He has been emotionally stronger. He is able to say, 'Okay, I've got Parkinson's. This is what it is. It is terrible, but I'm going to try to rise above it. For myself and for my family around me.'

Every day he wakes up and does that battle. I commend him for it.

He's getting the right treatment. He now has medication for the drop in blood pressure, so now he doesn't walk around woozy; he is off the random level of anxiety medications that he was taking. The situation is much more controlled and precise. Also, he is finally doing the right physiotherapy to address his physical problems, to maintain the abilities he has, rather than losing them. Speech therapy, to be able to be heard. This regime enables him to retain what he has.

On his last visit here to Israel at the end of 2019, we went to see the doctor he has been seeing for six years or so on his trips. The doctor said, 'I'm looking at my notes and seeing where you were several years ago, and you're better now.'

I know that Brian's neurologist in Sydney recently told him the same thing.

He is not getting better in terms of Parkinson's, but he is getting precise and accurate treatment and he is accepting what he has – acknowledging that he has Parkinson's and dealing with it.

This new approach adds to his ability to be positive. He knows what he has, rather than frantically searching and trying to understand. He's saying, 'I've got this condition and I'm going to move forward and do the best I can.'

Carrie

It was a real sense of relief to have the diagnosis. Brian seems much calmer and the anxiety feels like it has dissipated.

'Books, Books, Books!': Brian's Reflection on Gene's Academia (2021)

Drawing...On Darkness (2021)

Ondine's Compassionate Heart (2020)

2016

The neurology team that reviewed me in 2015 at the movement disorders clinic is top notch, but very far from my home, and the chief doctor's schedule is so busy he is inaccessible. I investigate options for settling on a treating doctor closer to where I live and work.

I am examined by a neurology group at a major teaching hospital. As with the previous session, I undergo a thorough examination, observed by multiple clinicians in a formal setting. They concur with their colleagues from further afield: I have mild to moderate PD.

The lead specialist, a very senior neurologist well regarded in his field, expresses his dismay that my original doctor adhered for so long to the view that I do not have Parkinson's. He does note, however, that my manifestation of PD is somewhat atypical. For example, I do not have a predominant tremor, nor do I have a great deal of dyskinesia, the jerky and uncontrollable body movements that plague some sufferers; rather, psychological symptoms such as anxiety and depression dominate. In relatively good news under the circumstances, he says that he feels my symptoms can be well managed to ensure the best possible quality of life. In his opinion, progression is likely to be extremely slow. There is some cause to be optimistic, to the extent that one can be.

I am confident in his abilities, and will continue to see this neurologist from here on in.

In terms of treatment, I believe Western medicine has clear limitations, and I am open to all possibilities. I decide to pursue alternative therapies that may support my wellbeing: acupuncture, kinesiology, herbal medicines, and injections of glutathione, a potent antioxidant, amongst other things. I also try Buteyko breathing, a breath control technique that is purported to improve psychological, emotional and physical health. Unfortunately, however, there is no really discernible long-term benefit.

I look into ice-cold water immersion therapy, which is claimed to enhance psychological and physical wellbeing when combined with meditation and breathing exercises, and meet with a leading international proponent of the method. However, it feels too radical and I decide against pursuing this path. At this time, too, my interest in the possibility of cannabis oil as a treatment is sparked, something I intend to pursue in due course.

There is some subtle critique from the medical fraternity because I am vegan, despite the fact that a balanced vegan diet is known to meet nutritional needs. I review my diet, consult a nutritionist and dietitian, and ensure my intake of vitamins, minerals and other nutrients is adequate.

This year, 2016, also coincides with an increase in my feeling of lower back and hip pain. It does not help, given that I am already struggling to deal with my various PD-related maladies. There was some question as to whether the compromised state of my mobility may be a function of an orthopedic problem, rather than PD. After rounds of examinations and scans, it is decided I will have keyhole surgery to decompress the joints in my lower back. The procedure is uneventful; just one more intervention in the roster of medical treatments that seem, now, to dominate my life.

I follow up later with cortisone injections, and a 'radiofrequency ablation' procedure to dull the pain. A fine needle is inserted into my lower spinal region, along which is passed an electrical current to burn the target nerves.

Thankfully, it provides relief for a time, and some months later I will have it done again, to keep the pain at bay.

WEDNESDAY, 1 JULY 2020

12pm, at the office having a coffee

Fortunately, my back and hip pain is much reduced due to the radiofrequency ablation I had on Saturday, a procedure I have now had several times.

It was eerie going to the hospital with very few people around (due to COVID). Gene and I arrived on time. Went to admissions, then waited for around three hours. Hard to remember the sequence of events. The anaesthetist put the injection into the top of my hand. Next thing I remember waking up and looking around for Gene, who was in the cubicle waiting for me. Ron picked us up a couple hours later and we were home. The procedure has eased the pain in my hip and back, which is a big relief.

Saturday midnight was my niece Danya's wedding in the US. Gene and I managed to stay up and be present for this occasion via Zoom. Sitting here right now, I literally feel as if I was in a chair in the room while Danya and Eli were getting married. Virtual reality? A very strange feeling; wonder if it's part of PD...

Brian Sherman's movement therapy (movement and hand–eye coordination exercises catching a ball), multiple exposure composite photograph by Gary Grealy

Ondine

'Devastating' would be the word I'd use. Dad has been suffering on an ongoing basis for, what, ten years or more. In terms of his description of how he has felt, it's almost like waking up every day with a terrible flu, and mostly people denying that you have it, or thinking that it's all in your head, and not knowing how to get better or if you'll ever get better, or not knowing what it even is. For so many years, he just was – we were all – in a state of total confusion and didn't really know what to do.

Dad's a problem-solving guy and someone who will put all his energy into attacking something, overcoming an obstacle or fighting a war, or whatever it is that he's focused on. He's like a pit bull – he grabs something and doesn't let go. He grabbed onto this. But in this case, I don't know if that personality trait really served him well, because he was just relentless in his pursuit of fixing himself. A lot of the time he approached his goal through taking medication after medication after medication. I remember at some point years ago, Gene going through the cabinets in their house and filling up bags and bags with bottles of medication that Dad had been trying and switching. He would play around with the quantities according to his mood on the day. I think a combination of his stubborn personality, which can be helpful in many circumstances, with his belief that there is a magic pill for any ailment, wasn't a good match in this situation.

Honestly, I blame the psychiatrists for wrongly over medicating him constantly. I think there was so much irresponsible and inappropriate prescribing, a lack of holistic oversight, of follow up, and of human to human connection. Dad believes in the medical profession and he trusts doctors. He goes to them to find solutions, and he follows their advice. I think this trust served him very badly.

Not one of those medications helped him. Eight years of constant medicating went by… I feel he was very hard done by and that people need to be careful or maybe something has to change in the system.

I think Dad went through mental, emotional and physical anguish during a long period of time, with none of us knowing what the answer was, or how to help him. And I guess having a clear diagnosis at least took away some of that anguish, and allowed him to settle down a little bit.

When he came to Israel for the boys' bar mitzvah at the end of 2019, there was a really big difference, in a positive way, between how he felt on this trip compared to when he came to Jasmine's bat mitzvah in mid 2016. He was not able to really interact with anybody during her celebrations. We had music and a big table outside with a beautiful buffet of vegan food. Dad was sitting inside on a couch the whole time. I said to him towards the end, 'Did you like the food? Did you eat anything?' He said, 'Oh, there was food? I didn't realise there was food.' He hadn't felt well enough to go outside, mingle, or even get himself a plate of food.

For the boys' bar mitzvah, the overwhelming feeling I got from him was that he was really proud that he had done the trip. I guess I didn't hear about the extent of his anxieties prior to travelling, but I know that he was exceptionally anxious. I was very determined that he get here, and wasn't giving him an out.

He often didn't feel good, and it was obviously hard for him to participate in things. But then again, he still has an amazing ability to form connections with people he doesn't know and make really strong impressions on them. So, for example, when he was here, I set him up with the boys' music therapist, Tomer. He's now doing drumming with Dad. I brought them together, and afterwards Tomer raved about Dad, saying what a special and amazing person he is, all the stuff that I would have felt might have been hard to see in Dad now because of his illness.

Obviously, he is still able to connect and form relationships with people without external help. That was very nice to see. And he enjoyed hanging around our house with the kids, just being present, for maybe five, six weeks.

At the time of Jasmine's bat mitzvah, Dad was on so much medication. He was out for the count, whereas at Dov and Lev's bar mitzvah, he was actually having conversations with people.

Now he is present and he is able to engage, because he is just taking what he needs to take for the Parkinson's.

Emile

The impact of the diagnosis itself was very good in that it gave certainty and a sort of identity to what Dad was suffering. He felt he knew what he had, and he could somehow galvanise himself around this as being the main reason for feeling the way he felt. The way his movements and physical phenomena were being experienced, now Parkinson's was to blame. I think it really helped to reduce anxiety, as he was then able to relax a bit.

At the same time, there were other stressors that came in to play. 'Oh, my God…I've got Parkinson's. This means certain things for my future.' And then anxiety set in about those things. But all in all, it was very good to have a diagnosis. There was a long time where it felt like Dad was almost willing himself to have Parkinson's. You have top specialists saying, 'You do not have Parkinson's, Brian.' One person would say, 'You may have some Parkinsonism.' Dad would hold on to that and say, 'Well, it's not for sure that I don't have it. I may have it.'

He would always over emphasise. One specialist said, 'You have incredibly light Parkinson's. It should not have any impact whatsoever on your life. You should be able to take pills and ride a bike and just live your life as though you were normal.' I was there in the meeting, and Dad came out saying, 'Yes, I've got proper Parkinson's.' There was a sense that he really wanted that diagnosis.

I would say, 'Dad, you know it's like you're willing yourself to have the disease. Well, do you want Parkinson's?'

And he'd say, 'Of course I don't.'

The reality is he does very much have it. So I think the diagnosis in the end, knowing what he has, is incredibly helpful and liberating.

I think the lowest point was in 2018, when Dad really started getting stuck in his movements. He went into hospital for observation to try to work things out, because nobody could get a handle on the situation. He would change pills. He was barely able to walk; couldn't walk to the end of the room.

I think that really scared everybody; he looked like he was on a steep downhill trajectory. He thought about death a lot at that time, as he's always done. We wanted to have a living will to make sure he didn't end up incapacitated and unable to make decisions about his end of life.

Now he's in a more stable, better place. His walking is clearly driven by the medication to a degree – he's doing the 'Parkinson's jog'. But his anxiety levels went down so much that he was able to make that trip to Israel in 2019 for Dov and Lev's bar mitzvah. He had a really good time and was better there than he was in Australia. There is a psychological component to this. Regardless of the fact that it is indisputable that Dad has Parkinson's, the mysteries of the mind meant that, in the right circumstances, he could bound out of bed.

Dror

In most ways, he is the same Brian. There's a layer of Parkinson's, whether it's physical or cognitive, like a cloud that he has to break through.

But he's the same person. I think, though, that he's become more in touch with his emotions. He'll tear up easily now. He's just more there emotionally, for better or for worse. It's not all cognitive. I think that's a positive thing. Maybe Brian still perceives crying sometimes as weakness, I'm not sure. But what it shows me is that he is more fully engaged in things around him.

He is deeply interested in family members. He is more focused on family, perhaps, than on the business side of things. I think he has found comfort in Emile to a large extent, in terms of being able to process the financial aspects, a certain sense that his legacy is being tended to. I mean not 100 per cent, I'm sure, but a lot more than two years ago. He had to give over.

I think it has been a positive process.

In general he has probably given over to those around him,

mostly family, I'd say, and those who are helping him, even staff who are also friends. He has given over and he is asking for assistance. I think that creates a closeness.

On the negative side, Brian's inability to talk makes it difficult to communicate over the phone. I'm sure it is hard for him. I really commend him for refusing to give up. He pushes through. But the inability to communicate verbally is difficult. Parts of his memory have become foggy and his ability to express himself has become patchy. These developments are certainly negative.

The really positive thing that happened when he was in Israel in 2019 was that I beat him in ping pong for the first time! So pleased I've been able to beat him. He still plays rather well.

'Hen': A Diptych: Free Expressive Painting (2021)

Abstract with Image of a Horse (2021)

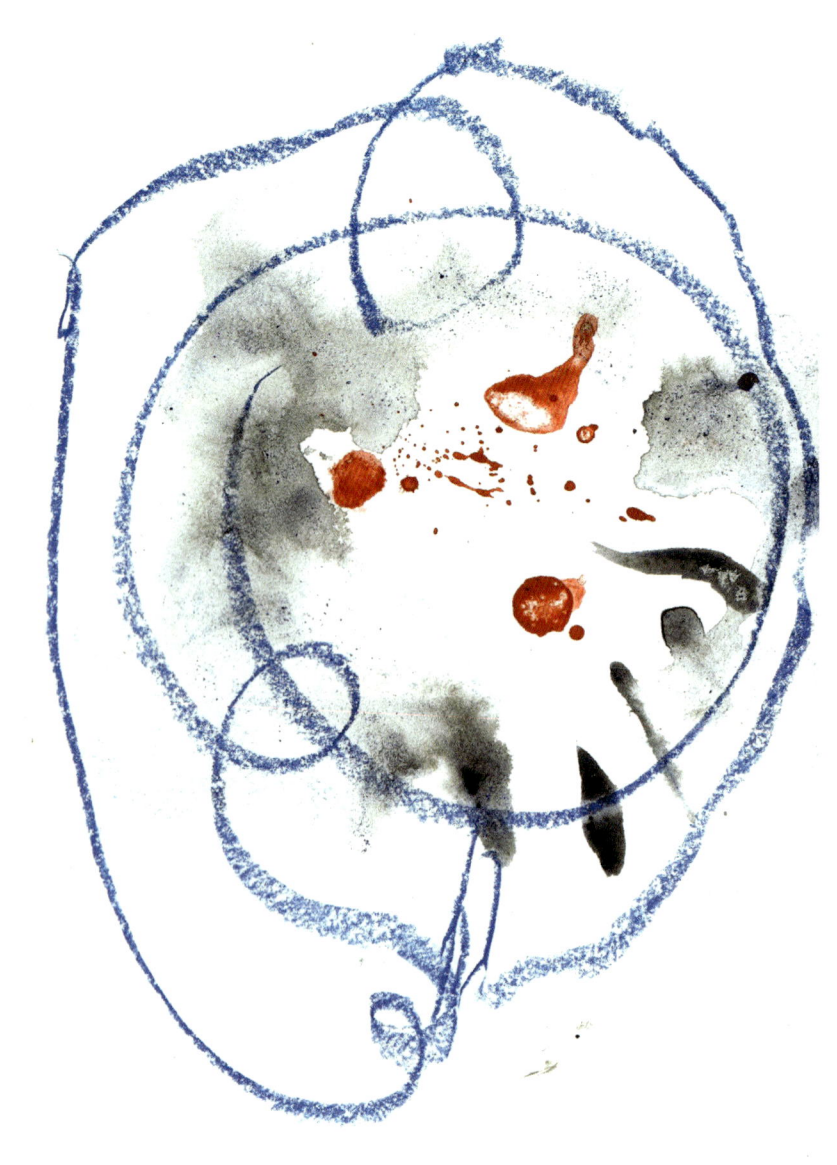

'Beauty Entangled': Brian's Abstract
of a Beautiful Girl (2021)

2017

As one year turns into the next, on the Parkinson's front I continue to struggle. It is curious, also, that my original specialist is yet to come to the conclusion that I definitely have Parkinson's. After an appointment in late February, he writes: *'Examining him from the Parkinson's point of view, it is always difficult to be sure whether he has Parkinson's or not.'*

Nevertheless, the weight of medical opinion is heavily on the side of PD, and my wellbeing is severely compromised. I decide to act on my interest in giving medical cannabis oil a shot.

While the jury is out, there is some evidence that for certain sufferers, medicinal cannabis has benefits for motor symptoms, psychological symptoms and the dyskinesia that can be induced by levodopa. In fact, there is copious documentation on the internet of its impacts. Videos show patients with uncontrollable dyskinesia and tremor taking small doses of the oil, after which their symptoms completely resolve. Numerous medical experts with credible affiliations to major universities endorse the benefits of medical cannanbis.

Gene has also read that it is a healing wonder medicine, and is quite convinced it would help both with my anxiety and my PD. She believes I have suffered so much for so long now that we must take steps to procure it, in the hope that it delivers some relief.

In Australia, access to cannabis for therapeutic purposes is notoriously difficult, even when the medical need is clearly established. My GP at the time had a patient who had procured cannabis from a 'wellness centre' in regional New South Wales run by a medical doctor.

My process begins with an intake form found on the centre's website, after which we receive a phone call seeking more information on my condition and needs. The centre follows up with a detailed 'prescription' for my treatment.

They recommend a three-step program for increasing quality of wellbeing, which includes a nutritional protocol. It involves removing sugar, carbs, dairy and alcohol from the diet, using only bottled water, and taking hemp seeds, acai berry powder and essential oils. As for the cannabis oil, the centre prescribes two versions: one containing CBD, or cannabidiol, which does not produce the high known to be associated with cannabis; and one predominantly THC, the psychoactive component. The latter is to be taken in the evening. In combination, the CBD moderates the THC 'high'.

We wait some time for the package to arrive in the mail. Gene manages to get in touch with the doctor late at night and tears strips off him for the delay. Soon, there is a parcel in the post.

I begin the regimen as prescribed, gradually increasing the dosage drop by drop. At first, I notice I am more relaxed, less distressed and my anxiety is reduced. My nausea is somewhat diminished, my appetite is better, and I am sleeping more soundly. The oil, in effect, knocks me out. It also knocks out REM sleep, so my nights are dreamless.

As time goes by, the medical establishment is not convinced that its benefits outweigh the downsides. My psychiatrist thinks the treatment contributes to my feelings of extreme heaviness in the morning – now a constant problem, which reduces my ability to remain active and puts a dampener on my mood. It is a belief with which my neurologist concurs, and eventually, I will come off the cannabis.

WEDNESDAY, 3 JUNE 2020

12:40pm

It's a nice early winter day out there.

Last night was my first night with no medical cannabis oil. I decided to come off it post an appointment with my GP who suggested (like other doctors) that the oil could be contributing to my heaviness each morning, my sense of dragging myself around like a dead weight. I went to bed around 11:40pm but woke again at 1:45am and thought it was later the next morning. I did get back to sleep after talking to the carer. I am hoping that after a couple of weeks of no oil, I may start to feel lighter on awakening.

My left hip is painful for a little while early in my day, but it troubles me less after I have walked.

On a positive note, I have been coming into the office now each day for a couple of hours. It is good to be back in the swing, to the extent that I am able to.

However, on the downside, I am now having problems swallowing my pills. My swallowing reflex doesn't work so well anymore. I must try to take my meds together with a smoothie, juice or a spoonful of ice cream to help them go down. Oh, the joys of this disease!

WEDNESDAY, 24 JUNE 2020

Had a small change in meds. Reduced the strength of my Parkinsin's med, Stalevo, from 150mg to 125mg and increased the Apomine flow to 0.85 from 0.65mls to try to deal with the dyskinesia and the 'off' periods, which are very trying and traumatic.

Every time there is a shift/change/increase/reduction in medication, there are consequences. I was told by the Apomine nurse that I will most likely not feel great for a few days to a week as my body adjusts to the different dose. At the same time, the medical cannabis oil is still withdrawing from my system. The GP told me it takes a month or more to wash out.

The year 2017 is notable for me for another reason, initially unrelated to Parkinson's. In December, I have a routine blood test for PSA – prostate specific antigen. It is the standard marker for prostate cancer. My PSA is markedly elevated. A biopsy follows. I am referred to a specialist urologist for further review and management. The result is a bolt from the blue. The treating urologist writes:

> *I reviewed Brian today. His biopsy, which was performed on 19 December, shows…a significant tumour, which could be a problem within five to ten years, and even though he has a significant Parkinsonian disorder, I think it should be treated given the [tumour] score and the slow progression of the Parkinson's disease.*
>
> *I think that given his age, Parkinson's and his sensitivity to anaesthesia and the unacceptability of being incontinent, radiation is the best form of treatment. Assuming he agrees to that, I will [arrange for preparations in early February] with a view to having radiotherapy in mid-February 2018.*

There follows a referral to a radiation oncologist who specialises in the treatment of prostate cancer. I am assured the treatment will have absolutely no effect on my overall condition, and, to quote the words of the physician, 'no impact on my Parkinson's'. Perhaps I am the exception that proves the rule. Things take a turn for the worse.

THURSDAY, 2 JULY 2020

2:17pm

Beautiful warm winter's day. At home today, no office. Was a bit foggy in my therapy session. I've had a re-emergence of some pain in the right hip; not when I sit but when I walk or stand.

I'm feeling slow but the nausea is gone. Perhaps it helps that I am now drinking a shake when I take my first morning pills at about 8am. I also think the medical cannabis is finally seeping out of my system. My heaviness when I wake in the mornings is reduced. I keep waiting for it to return. It's been there for years, so it is hard to trust it's not going to come back.

COVID has gained momentum in Victoria. I think it's going to be here for a long time.

I'm not in the right space to write too much today. I have personal training at 2:30pm, and am seeing the specialist via Zoom tomorrow for a prostate check up and to discuss meds.

THURSDAY, 9 JULY 2020

2pm

I feel okay. My therapist suggested I should video myself doing some physical activities such as table tennis, swimming in summer, walking Miracle in the park, or with Neil doing personal training.

I am not sure the back procedure helped me this time – hard to know. I am still having back pain.

This really affects my ability to go for walks and to play table tennis, which is very disappointing.

On Monday, some of our staff came back to the office after four months of COVID-imposed working from home.

TUESDAY, 21 JULY 2020

11:30am

Yesterday afternoon I felt terrible – very tentative, anxious, as if I was in a whirl. Slight dizziness did not help. I took half a Serepax, which eased things a bit.

My back is still sore, especially when I go for a long walk – long now being to the end of the block and back.

About a week ago, I had a dream that Iran joined forces with China. Iran supplied China with oil and China used Iran as a forward military base. Israel is vulnerable because Trump is undercutting it. Australia joins Israel and China takes over Australia. It felt very real.

Two days later there was an article in the *Jewish News* saying that China and Iran have a comprehensive agreement for working together. I felt like I had a premonition.

Carrie

In the beginning, Brian had a sense of hopelessness. He was talking to everyone about PD. There were so many different diagnoses, so many doctors. Gene, Emile, Ondine and Dror were continuously involved and on the journey with him, as Brian looked for a new avenue and new opinions, never giving up.

He feels so much calmer, and more accepting of his situation now. Brian is an incredible person; his old routine is gone, and he just gets on with the ordinary aspects of everyday life and is even learning new things, such as painting and drumming. He intuitively takes on new challenges.

Ondine

Dad is more settled. We've come to understand that there is not all that much to be done except what he is doing. The panic around finding what's wrong with him, seeing doctors and having constant tests has subsided. That's an improvement. I wonder if the shift is simply circumstantial or if he really has changed inwardly. I don't think he has changed.

I guess becoming more self-aware is a positive thing, and maybe he has improved at this level. However, I don't think he has gone through a major spiritual awakening. He was a good guy to begin with.

A lot of the traits he had, which have served him well, were really good traits. They've helped him to achieve the things he's achieved, to be dogged in his determination, and, definitely with regard to Voiceless and animals, to make a difference. It is obvious that some things in life you have to surrender to; there are things you can't change, you can't beat. I'm not sure whether Dad has come to a greater realisation of this. Maybe a little. Maybe…

Emile

I definitely think there is a sense of acceptance and peace. Dad did shift a couple of years ago, and even more maybe a year ago, where he was suffering less during the day. For so many years he was suffering terribly.

This is why I really don't believe his situation was all related to Parkinson's. His condition was Parkinson's related, but not Parkinson's caused, in the sense that there were clearly other genuine psychological forces at play. He was in a state of terror during the day and in absolute psychological pain and torment, not really able to sit still or be in his own skin. That has calmed down. Dad is much calmer and I think the Parkinson's has stabilised.

The physical side, the anxiety, the Parkinson's related anxiety or depression, has all stabilised and he has stabilised in a place that is not super happy. He's not feeling good a lot of the time. On the other hand, there are times when he does feel good, and to be honest, before any of the symptoms presented themselves, he wasn't in a great emotional place. I think if we took Parkinson's out of the picture, I'm not quite sure how much better Dad would be emotionally.

I mean, he definitely would be better emotionally, and probably substantially, but exactly how much is hard to determine.

There is no doubt that Dad is significantly affected by Parkinson's. Even with the pills he is taking, his movement is very affected. He's had some cognitive decline, which I understand is an effect of Parkinson's. Again, I don't know how much that would have happened naturally. But his speech is much softer; he has blood pressure issues. Parkinson's is having a big impact on his experience of being in the world, on his being, his body and his head. At the same time, he's not in such a terrible physical condition. He can move. We play ping pong.

Timeless (2021)

Circle of Time (2021)

Mood Changes II: 'Willy, Willy' (2021)

2018

The prostate cancer treatment involves some preparatory rigamarole, none of it pleasant.

I have a specialised PET scan to determine if the cancer has metastasised. Radioactive dye is injected into my vein in preparation for the imaging procedure. The tracer dye tracks the presence of prostate cancer cells throughout the body. If the original tumour has spread, cells in affected regions, such as the bones or lymph nodes, light up on scanning. On this count, the news is a relief. The test shows no evidence of metastasis. Radiotherapy targeted only to the prostate may proceed as planned.

First, I am required to have a small surgical procedure: the placement of fiducial markers. These are tiny pellets of gold, about the size of a grain of rice. They are inserted into the prostate to guide the radiation therapy to the regions affected by the tumour, and to minimise radiation damage to surrounding tissue. Gold is many more times dense on X-ray than steel, so provides the radiologist with the best visual target. At the same time, I have a SpaceOAR Hydorgel procedure. Gel is placed between the rectum and the prostate to separate the two and help protect the rectum from radiation.

I am given a light general anaesthetic. Then the doctors insert tiny needles into my prostate, through which the markers and gel are inserted. Afterwards, I have a feeling of fullness in the area, but no ill effects.

One week later, I have a planning scan, which enables the radiation oncologist to direct the treatment with the highest degree of accuracy. Radiation begins a week later again. I will be treated Monday to Friday for around seven weeks. The procedure itself is short, with the radiation beam operating for only 90 seconds.

I am reassured that I will feel nothing, except toward the end of the treatment there will be some inflammation in the base of the bladder, possible stinging on urination, and the need to empty my bladder more often. This can be treated with cranberry juice. The advice is that I may become more fatigued around the end of the treatment as well, with residual tiredness afterwards, but I should continue my usual exercise regime and schedule of work and appointments.

The radiation, in short, should not affect me much at all. On the contrary, I am told, if I do not undergo it and leave the tumour as is, it will metastasise and potentially grow into the bladder and rectum, causing massive pain. I may need bags for both. The doctor's strong view is there is a window right now to treat the cancer and shrink the tumour. The only other option is hormone therapy, but he does not recommend it. It could come with too many serious and unpleasant side effects, and it may cause a worsening of my current condition.

I begin the course of radiotherapy in a positive mindset, with respect to the treatment at least. I have no reason to doubt the oncologist's reassurances.

The first week or so goes reasonably to plan. I feel nothing, other than the usual ravages of Parkinson's.

Soon enough, though, there is a radical shift. I have the sensation that I am declining fast, into a black hole of escalating infirmity. After five treatments, I am teetering on the brink; after ten, I am a rapidly disappearing vestige of my former already diminished self.

Exhaustion envelopes me. I am frail, hardly able to walk, and my speech is reduced to a whisper. I start to experience the severe 'freezing' episodes that characterise worsening Parkinson's. My feet stick to the floor as if held there by an immovable weight. I have some dyskinesia, the jerky, uncoordinated movements of the typical PD sufferer. I am going downhill fast, and am desperate to arrest the slide.

My condition is unsustainable; the radiotherapy is stopped after ten of the scheduled 34 sessions. I am admitted to a large teaching hospital to be stabilised. There follows another period at a rehabilitation hospital. My condition is treated more wholistically, but when I return home, I am still decrepit. My worsened condition persists. A decision is made that I should return to the teaching hospital for further stabilisation. In all, I am admitted for some five weeks.

To say it is a rough patch is the understatement of the century. My mental condition is precarious. At this time, the psychological torment I have been enduring goes into overdrive. My stream of consciousness notes – jumpy, discontinuous, black, despairing – track the jagged contours of my deterioration.

Easter weekend, 2018

THE FINAL PUSH

I am overwhelmed, confused.
    I don't know what I need, what's going to help me.
    I know what I want to say but can't get the words out.
    Memories come in and out of focus.
    A plea from the other me – locked inside...
    It's morning and the night has passed. Inch by inch, centimetre by centimetre, my life force, my being is being eroded and then, presto, the heavy veil covering my face slowly lifts. I know that I am slowly disappearing. The Brian Sherman you all once knew will be no more.

    I am desperate to get my autobiography. It is done, save for process, which is still substantial. Please, please take an executive decision, print, publish and distribute. The waiting is indescribable.

    The book is a time capsule for my grandchildren. To encourage them to make a contribution. I want to give the grandchildren a sense of our family history and of the continuity of history.

* * *

I can't describe my agony let alone communicate it to you.

PD is different for each sufferer. Mine now feels aggressive. On looking back, a lot of the symptoms I previously experienced, such as feeling spacey, dizzy, especially in the mid-mornings, can be attributed to PD. Depression and anxiety too (not exclusively so).

My dreams range from torrid nightmares to intellectual and strategic ways of tackling contracts, partnerships, relationships, the bulk of which stem from interaction between the various medications I take as well as a newly discovered blood pressure issue – the differential between low and high blood pressure that has me all over the shop.

Afternoons, I don't know what to do – jump out of my skin? I am slower and heavier, suffering extreme exhaustion.

I am scared of taking a nap, afraid of feeling worse, fearful of being locked into my body, watching it but unable to move, unable to snap out of the dead weight of my state of being, my lethargy.

We are united in our common humanity. No one is immune from grief.

The mistreatment of animals…factory farms are a crime. We gave voice to the Voiceless.

I want to shine a light on human suffering too.

* * *

My urine is reddish copper in colour – has been like this for some weeks.

My body, for the past few weeks, heats up. Yet my toes are freezing cold – bad circulation.

Uncomfortable disturbed sleep, turbulent. I wake up every 45–60 minutes and get anxious. Watch the time continuously; go to sleep 11pm, wake at 11:45pm and think it's the next day. Think I slept more than ten hours but it's less than one.

Very conscious of my feet – getting cramps. Need to keep my feet higher than my body.

I feel that my brain is starved of oxygen.

Need to go to the loo to urinate but can't walk well. Feet sticking to ground. Progressing pitifully inch by inch. No falls but close to it. Wearing stockings for compression. Go four to five times per night to no avail.

Am I getting (more) depressed?

What happens if I go to the opera or a movie and can't get up?

If I focus on a movie/ TV/emails/discussion, I feel a little better.

It is a struggle to read books, newspapers, etc. My ultra short-term memory is failing, or is it lack of interest, given the big picture? When I wake at night it is difficult to read the info board in the hospital, let alone a book.

The sole of my right foot gives me pain most of the time.

Easter Sunday

Added a new drug – Quetiapine. Won't help to get me to sleep but will help in keeping me asleep, I am told. It's antipsychotic, used for schizophrenia/bipolar and major depressive disorder. Shake me and I'd rattle.

Easter Monday

Difficult morning. Woke during the night. Torrid nightmare.

Rang nurse 2–4am – can't remember – and went to loo. Awake again at 6am. Very anxious. Pill took an hour to kick in.

Spoke to Lloyd in tears. Can't carry on.

Walk with Emile, Carrie and the boys.

Back 1:30pm

Lunch pill 1:30pm

Living with PD = battle.

Like my focus on MCT8 – a rare and genetically debilitating disorder afflicting my grandsons.

Trying to come to terms with life.

No one is immune from its slings and arrows. Family, people you love...

The irony of my last entry from that time, about looking on the bright side, does not escape me.

Notwithstanding my anguish, while in hospital there is a watershed. Review of my medication – key to one's state of being in PD – puts me on a more even keel. The doctors change me from one form of levodopa to another, and then to another, which will prove important in my ongoing recovery from this sudden and precipitous decline. The new drug, apomorphine, is administered by infusion via a small pump attached to the fatty tissue of the abdomen. The advantage is that it keeps the blood level of dopamine more constant, ironing out the highs and lows that can affect the severity of one's PD symptoms and quality of life.

The good news is, as the apomorphine comes into effect, I get a little better. In retrospect, it was a turning point.

THURSDAY, 30 JULY 2020

2:10pm

I am having a better day today. It's been a stressful week.

On Monday, I went for my follow-up appointment with the specialist who did my back ablation procedure. After a 45-minute wait, he gave me four minutes of his time.

I explained that I'm still in pain, and he prescribed a 'light' muscle relaxant. He told me to come back in three months and have the ablation procedure again if I am not better.

I duly take the pill.

By 6pm, Gene notices I am not myself. I am dazed, out of it. That night, I'm confused, and I struggle to orient myself. I'm shaky and cold and I've lost the sense of my body in space. The carer says she has never seen me like that. It is fortunate I do not fall or injure myself.

I go to see the GP the next day, who confirms the problem is the medication; the relaxant is most likely interacting with another of my drugs. It takes me two days to feel my 'normal' self. I don't touch that pill again.

It is a lesson. I'm on multiple PD drugs, and another med cannot simply be added to the mix without careful consideration of the effects. The doctor did not care two hoots, and failed to do his homework. I hate to think of what may have happened if I did not have the level of attention and care I do at home.

THURSDAY, 6 AUGUST 2020

11:48am

Beautiful day. Had a good walk this morning with a friend. My lower back is generally feeling a bit better.

Am starting a new medication, Ebixa, to improve memory function. Will see how that goes.

Last night I went to see a movie with Gene at a local cinema. We are still in COVID times and the theatre was near empty; only two other people. It is good to be out in the world a bit, to the extent that I am able.

My sleeping without the cannabis oil has been reasonably good. I am waking approximately three times per night and propel myself to the bathroom on the walking frame. During the day I tend to use my walking stick. I don't always need it, but if I go for a proper walk, it gives me extra stability.

MONDAY, 13 AUGUST 2020

3:30pm

Feeling not too bad today. Had no vivid dreams or nightmares last night. Generally speaking, my back is a little better, but I need to go for a long walk to really tell.

Mood is around six out of ten; an advance on previously, when it has often hovered at barely above zero.

There's another turn for the better. A year or two ago, I could not read the newspapers; it was impossible to focus on more than one to two lines at a time. Now I can read articles from beginning to end. This an unexpected improvement from within the maelstrom of my illness.

Another bonus: my table tennis ability is stable. Amazingly, those deep-seated, long established reflexes remain intact as other aspects of my physical capacity crumble.

Will try tennis at some point again, maybe with Emile, and see how that goes. Started art therapy yesterday, one-on-one sessions with an art therapist. I'm willing to explore various issues through drawing and painting.

Who knows what will emerge from the depths of my psyche?

Gene

There is deterioration. There will be, there has been, there is and there still will be. But after Brian's hospitalisation for six weeks in 2018, his doctor felt that the delicate balance of this pill and that pill – and Brian swallowed God knows how many pills a day – had been very well achieved, particularly with the apomorphine, which proved to be a huge breakthrough intervention.

I remember very clearly the conversation with his neurologist in the corridor of the hospital in 2018, talking about apomorphine. He said, 'Gene, it is a real bother because the needle needs to be inserted and then taken out, daily; you need special nurses...'

I said, 'I don't care how much of a bother it is, if it has a chance of working, let's try it.'

Within days it made, I think, a significant difference to Brian.

He can't walk to the main street now, and he could do that six months ago. The change is partly because of his gait; his bent-over posture is causing back pain now. It is clear to the naked eye that his back is not aligned properly. This is a recent, big disappointment, for me and for Brian, in that we bought this house so we could go for long walks in Centennial Park. He can't do that anymore. The situation has changed after living a year in the house; he could walk in the park when we moved in.

The other thing – I'll cite the bad things first and then the good things – the other thing that makes it difficult for me is his typical-for-Parkinson's speech. It has become slurry and has changed his voice. Since Parkinson's truly kicked in, his voice has progressively become softer.

My hearing is not as it should be; just old age, I am 74.

He is having regular speech therapy. If I say to him, 'Speak up, darling, I can't hear you,' he does so; the effort is huge, but he can't sustain or maintain the volume.

The two really difficult things from my point of view are the walking and speaking. On the positive side, what I have found – and there have been ups and downs with this – is that his memory remains relatively good.

As we know, everybody loses memory as they age. I think he has pills now that have helped, or perhaps the general stability of the pills has created an improvement. His memory is actually fine for his age, he can remember anything he needs to remember.

Moreover, his wisdom is still perfect. He invariably comes up with just the right solution for any and all problems the rest of us are debating – a family issue or a staffing issue or perhaps a dog issue, and he'll come up with a comment, and everybody agrees that the way to go has suddenly become clear.

Emile

Dad's emotional state over the last fifteen years cannot be reduced to Parkinson's.

I think there is a view now that one can read the whole saga as a manifestation of Parkinson's – the psychological side, the anxiety and depression and the emotional nature of it all. But for me, I think there has been a whole range of issues, and a psychological stream that was happening well before Parkinson's started presenting itself. I think this meant that Dad was ill-equipped emotionally to deal with Parkinson's. It might have even precipitated it. I don't know.

I remember being told by neurologists that Parkinsonian-type conditions can come about through significant stress in life. The obsession that Dad took on to find the diagnosis and cure for Dov and Lev ended up being too much for him. He couldn't process what had happened emotionally and his body collapsed. I don't know.

The big question with Dad is that interplay between the psychological and physiological, and his relentless focus on his condition, on the mystery of what it is and how to solve it. Does that exacerbate the condition itself? That's the core question.

He has been in therapy for many, many years, but somehow he has not sufficiently developed the mental tools which might allow him to reduce his obsessing. I don't know if he wants to let go, to be honest. I think it's part of his identity, that tenacious 'I'm not going to let go. I'd almost be a failure if I stopped obsessing.' It's how he has approached everything in his life, and he's not about to stop doing that with Parkinson's, which he sees as his final mountain. So this journey is, I think, part of the same paradigm as EquitiLink, or Voiceless, or Dov and Lev.

But how much is his focus on the Parkinson's helping him and how much is it hurting him? This is a really core question.

Ondine

It has been hard and sad and difficult to see your alpha-male patriarch, who has always looked after you, become very vulnerable and feel incapable of functioning. The situation emotionally has been very difficult, but I guess I'm trying to look at the positive side.

I've now seen different sides of Dad's character that I probably wouldn't have seen. Seeing someone in an emotional, vulnerable state, you get to know them in a different way, and you can try to be there for them and care for them, which is good to be able to do. If someone you love stays in your mind as a powerful person and you never, ever, see any weakness, your view of them doesn't really fully reflect their human condition.

Unholy Mess (2021)

Untitled ('Timeless') (2021)

Flying Low (2021)

2019

It's groundhog year, again.

My disease is my constant companion. I understand it will never leave my side. Yet the months that follow are an improvement on the year past. With some bumps along the way, I am largely in a holding pattern, trying to prevent the slide.

Of enormous help in my journey has been my longtime psychotherapist. For a protracted period, in the absence of any firm diagnosis of PD, it was reasonable to assume my symptoms were related to depression and anxiety; that was my thinking, and my family and others largely concurred. My therapist's support through all those years of turmoil and unknowing was a godsend. I still have sessions each week. Sometimes, Gene joins me, and together we confront some of the issues surrounding my struggle with PD.

Sessions are a moment of reflection free from the hubbub and busy work of managing my disease, a quiet space behind the scenes. The therapy brings a new lens to my thinking, enabling me to look at my situation from a fresh perspective inaccessible to me when left to my own devices. Over the years, the therapeutic relationship has deepened, and I can genuinely say I have derived long-term benefits that go well beyond the tangible.

Therapy has taken me back to my childhood, which was very repressed, and brought many a smile to my face. It has given me a sense of my life as whole – of my personhood in the fullest sense – and insight into how and why I became the person that I am. It is ironic that I have come to know myself better just as I slowly lose the self I once was.

This year, I also embark on a couple of new treatments. One is TMS, transcranial magnetic stimulation. According to the research, it is meant to have therapeutic benefits for PD, potentially alleviating both motor and mood symptoms, including depression.

At the TMS clinic, my apomorphine pump is removed, and I am asked to leave my phone outside the treatment room, as the TMS equipment may affect machinery and wipe data. I am ushered in for the session and settled in a chair next to the device. Electrodes are fixed to my head for the procedure, through which magnetic impulses will be delivered to my brain. I'm told I'll experience very little, if anything, in terms of sensations.

It seems I buck the norm. With each pulse, I feel a severe electric shock. It is deeply unpleasant, but I persist. The intention is that I have an extensive series of sessions, three lots of ten days, but it is too painful. I have one more session, but cannot tolerate it, so cancel the remaining appointments.

I am not ready to give up on TMS completely, though. I try the treatment again, at the clinic of a highly regarded medical specialist who is also a friend, and who has been a great support and source of advice to me. The electrodes are placed differently, and the level of vibration I experience as the pulses are administered is much reduced. After the first two sessions, I feel what I think is some overall improvement in my state of being, like I am better connecting the dots. I continue for a few more sessions, but overall, if there is any change, it is negligible. I hasten to add that this is my experience. Others may derive benefit where I have not. Everything in this condition is so individual.

Next cab off the rank is red light therapy, again, purported to have benefits for motor and nonmotor PD symptoms, mainly via controlling the circadian rhythms that regulate the sleep–wake cycle. We buy the red light from overseas, and my carer administers the treatment. I stand facing the light in my underclothes and rotate. I persist for twenty minutes every second day, then every day, for a couple of months. There is no effect.

It's disappointing that these treatments provide no relief, but nothing ventured, nothing gained.

This year, I'm dealing with one particularly unstable symptom. My blood pressure is all over the shop and is vulnerable to any change in medications. At one point, I am prescribed a Parkinson's related medication at too high a level. It over stimulates my heart and I have a hypertensive crisis that lands me in the emergency department. I am stabilised overnight and discharged the next day. There are no lasting effects, but over the months my BP continues to fluctuate, and I experience low blood pressure episodes. When this happens, I need to lie down on the floor with my lower legs elevated on a stack of books, until normal pressure is restored.

Overall though, in comparison to my previous state, there are hints of improvement, relatively speaking, or at least stabilisation, despite the progressive nature of my condition.

* * *

It's late 2019, and Dov and Lev's bar mitzvah in Israel is not long away. Ondine and Dror strongly encourage me to attend, but I am deeply apprehensive. Of course, I would love nothing more than to be there for my grandsons, but I worry about how I will manage every aspect of the journey, not least the long-haul flights. I am fortunate that I have extensive assistance, and decide to proceed.

Dov and Lev are thirteen. They are happy and dearly loved. Although the boys are nonverbal and unable to sit, crawl or walk independently, their *joie de vie* is apparent from their smiles and actions.

Family has come from all over for the momentous event. Alongside Gene and me are my brother Ron and his wife, Mary, their daughter Danya and her then fiancé, now husband, Eli, Dror's family, and Emile and Carrie and their kids, Milo, Zachy and Cy.

The night before, there is a vegan feast at Dror and Ondine's family home around a huge communal table. It had been bucketing down all day, and the plans to hold the dinner in a marquee outside are shelved. The deluge doesn't dampen anyone's spirits. The boys love communal singing, and the family and guests join in with gusto. There are heartfelt speeches and good cheer all around. In my limited way, I participate to the best of my ability. It is good to be surrounded by my happy, loving family, celebrating the boys' transition to young adulthood.

The next day is the bar mitzvah. I look outside, and the skies have opened. The deluge has turned biblical. But when we go to the synagogue just around the corner from Ondine and Dror's house, the rain miraculously stops.

Dov and Lev are frequent attendees at this synagogue. They go each Friday night, usually with Dror, and on Saturdays with their carers, who wait on a bench in the garden outside. They love the rabbi, and greatly enjoy the rituals and the sense of independence. They're happy to spend long periods there, fully engaged and absorbed.

The synagogue is orthodox, so there is usually a separation between men and women, with the women behind a curtain on a raised platform. Dror and Ondine had negotiated with the rabbi in the months beforehand to take the curtain out for the event, and to move some of the prayers closer to where the women usually sit.

The boys are fully prepared and keen participants in every minute of the proceedings. With the touch of a button, they activate the Torah prayers, which had been recorded beforehand, and the place fills with mellifluous chanting. Guests are called up to recite prayers, the men wearing tallit, the white prayer shawls; and since it is Hanukkah, some of the women are given the duty of lighting the Hanukkah candles.

There is live music, with a violinist and keyboardist, which adds to the ambience and sense of occasion. Dror and Ondine had prepared a video showing Dov and Lev and their interests, scenes from their lives, and people offering congratulations on the bar mitzvah, and they play it on a large screen. The place is packed full, with more than a hundred people, and the boys are the stars of the show. It is deeply affecting.

Celebrations continue outside. A vegan brunch is served, which the many guests enjoy as they mill around and talk. Dov and Lev's music therapist creates a drumming circle and the boys are in their element, transported by the sound.

I am transported, too. Coming to Israel was the right decision. I cope well, and am pleased that even in my dilapidated state, I still have it in me to participate. It has been a balm to spend time with Ondine, Dror, the boys and Jasmine. Incredibly, I end the decade in a better state than I started it.

MONDAY, 24 AUGUST 2020

3:40pm

It's been a hard weekend. On Friday, I lost my best friend, my dog Miracle. She was about twelve years old and walking in the park with Martha, our dog walker, when she had a sudden heart attack. She passed away then and there.

I went to the vet hospital and sat with her for a few hours. I held her and said goodbye. The house feels empty without her.

We were inseparable. She had been with me, literally at my side, through my entire Parkinson's journey. It is a shock, and I mourn the loss of her. She leaves a gap in my life, and in my heart.

Brian Sherman's movement therapy (Brian walking at a slow and medium pace with weights – in profile), multiple exposure composite photograph by Gary Grealy

Gene

I think every Western doctor agrees now that one's emotional life and one's physical life are intertwined.

Because we are so different, so finely tuned, both as human beings and because we all come with genetic predispositions and with emotional baggage from our childhoods, you can never say one and one makes two, or that this predisposition or that parental input leads to a specific outcome.

Clearly, Brian overdid things during the EquitiLink roadshow years. Nobody could possibly say that he and Laurence didn't overwork. Laurence ended up with heart bypasses and Brian constantly gulped down antibiotics so as to override flu.

Those roadshows, however, gave us significant opportunities. For me, the opportunity to have the Sherman Contemporary Art Foundation (SCAF) and Sherman Centre for Culture and Ideas (SCCI), for Emile the opportunity to kick-start a film production house, for Ondine to follow her passion with Voiceless, and for the politicians and journalists who went on Rambam, a thousand of them at least, the opportunity to visit the Middle East and see the situation first-hand.

The roadshows and the financial success that followed in their wake had a huge positive impact on the family, on our lifestyle, on our freedom, on our ability to choose what we wanted to do, on our philanthropic endeavours. One cannot underestimate the positive consequences of that super demanding period, when the money was made by the sweat of their brows. However, believing that there were no negative consequences would, I think, simply be illogical. One can't measure the downside. We are talking about a period of fifteen years intensive work, not five months.

Carrie

Brian is the most caring, wonderful father-in-law and grandfather. To see him struggle in the beginning was incredibly sad. I feel hopeful now, since he has found a way of being in the present and just spending time with the family.

We all adore spending time with him. Brian is just the most accepting, non-judgmental, wise and easy presence to be around. Even in a state of panic and confusion, he always manages to come up with an insightful comment, and often gets right to the heart of the matter.

We love nothing more than having Brian over on a Tuesday night. The boys can spend quality time with Papa. And he still often beats one of them at table tennis.

He likes to listen intently to their conversations and often tears up when the boys tell him a story. Brian is always on my side when it comes to chores and manners. Raising three boys is a handful; it is a drop easier when he is around. Brian was the first of the boys' grandparents to change a nappy. We even travelled together to Italy via Bangkok with Brian pacing up and down the aisles of the plane with Milo (now fifteen) when he was four months old.

He remains the wonderful person he always was.

Emile

Dad's journey has been all-encompassing, involving everyone in the family, obviously. My mum is living with him every day and, for many years, his illness has dominated their marriage in so many ways. And for me, over the last eleven or twelve years, my relationship with him has been largely defined around Parkinson's. There have been moments of true crisis, where I've felt like we were dealing with somebody who was potentially suicidal.

To be around somebody on an ongoing basis who is psychologically suffering has been challenging. Plenty of people can have limited physical movements. You could be in a wheelchair and be happy.

I would constantly ask myself, 'How is Dad? How is he feeling?' Energy flows from me to him. He has always been, and still is an incredibly generous father, incredibly un-egotistical, incredibly un-self-obsessed. Until Parkinson's came along, Dad continued to be deeply interested in what I do and wanted to hear about me. There is no doubt, though, that an enormous vortex of energy has been expended, trying to help Dad manage the process, his emotional state, his sense of a future, his anxieties, the psychological, the medication and also the physical, neurological side.

The kids are very involved in Dad and Mum's lives and vice versa. They have grown up with everyone asking, 'How is Papa? How is he doing? Is he okay?' You know, this has been a really big part of our conversations about their grandfather. I think Dad feels sad that he's not able to be the grandfather who plays tennis with the kids, runs around with them in the park and is more active and more present. That said, he is unbelievably present with them, but his illness is a presence as well. It has really been there in the room during the course of their whole lives.

The relief now is that he doesn't seem to be suffering psychologically as much as he was before. I think his biggest journey has been the incredible psychological vortex into which he has descended.

Before all of this, I had never really seen Dad cry. He was always such a strong presence in my life. He is certainly a lot more emotional now – which is quite nice.

I think this generally happens as one gets older. But it is particularly acute in his case. If there is an emotional moment in the family, in a film, or whatever, Dad will respond and become tearful.

His illness has, of course, affected my relationship with him massively. We have a hugely loving, close relationship. I feel very, very dutiful in that I need to make sure that he is okay.

Dror

It's painful to see Brian suffer, and to see the physical difficulty, the emotional difficulty, the hardship involved in communication. I feel pain and sadness for him. He's such a dynamic person and such a proactive person, and we have a wonderful relationship

– not only through values but also via our adventures together, cycling, walking, trekking.

Working on a diagnosis and treatment for the boys, he was really active. And he still is to some degree, but no longer all the way.

Together we worked on the first two-thirds of focused research – trying to find a cure for the boys. He could then engage actively and purposefully. There has been a big loss – I lost a partner. His decline forced me to step up, I guess.

It has been sad. On the other hand, I feel a huge amount of respect for Brian, for his tenacity and his ability to deal with adversity.

He doesn't give up. I constantly find that I'm learning lessons from him. I learnt from him in the past and I learn lessons now seeing how he deals with a personal, physical crisis.

If I become afflicted in a similar way, I hope that I will stay positive towards my family and friends. Brian has made a huge internal journey trying to be positive for the family, for people he is close to. He works at it, constantly trying. And I really, really admire him for it.

Even the act of working on this book is typical Brian. He is trying to make himself better and to find treatments for his condition – and then decides to do a book so as to make others more aware of what Parkinson's is like. He's putting his experience out there for everybody to see, to raise awareness.

He is doing a wonderful thing. I feel full of admiration. His voice is quiet but his actions are very loud. This book is part of that.

Abstract Man and His Dog (2021)

A Day at the Dentist (2021)

Emile

I'm a big believer in holding on to the silver linings of adversity. And sometimes, often even, pain, challenges and vulnerability truly do make better people. But the reality here is that Parkinson's has been bad for Brian. He wasn't an egotistical, disconnected man, a bad father or husband or boss, who through Parkinson's has learned humility and interconnectedness. Dad has always been a wonderful man. Very kind, very generous, very tenacious, very focused, very loving and family-orientated. And he is the same now, but with Parkinson's making so much of his life a struggle. This is not a story of redemption by Parkinson's.

That said, the disease has continued to reveal and deepen his qualities. He has not become bitter and overtly angry or nasty. He hasn't given up, either.

If there's one identifiable thing that has shifted, towards the positive, it is that he has embraced vulnerability. Dad was never very vulnerable. He was physically and mentally strong, or at least he seemed so to me as his son. He never cried. And for many men, particularly those of his generation, being hit with something like Parkinson's can feel shameful. They pretend they're okay, and don't want to admit to vulnerabilities. Dad has done the opposite. He has not hidden in shame. He is out and proud, even if somewhat tearful. But he asks for help, and he is so very open about how he is feeling and about his limitations. In our culture, which is only now coming to terms with these things, Dad is a real trailblazer, particularly for older men. I know he has had a big impact on many men who have felt unable, or nervous about admitting to their vulnerabilities.

Another positive – he seems to be fighting himself less. Before Parkinson's, he was in a state of anxiety and depression. Maybe that was partly due to Parkinson's, but he certainly was in a state of turmoil. He has calmed now and is more at ease. I don't really know if Parkinson's was the poison or the cure, but to the extent that it has helped him relax, it has been a relatively good thing.

Aside from this small consolation, his situation is pretty shit.

Ondine

Today I see Dad as fully human – not a powerhouse and problemsolver and parent, but as a person who is vulnerable, sad, scared and needs support like we all do. I'd never seen him cry before – and seeing a parent express raw emotion like that has been helpful in my own life, to know that it is okay.

Despite his terrible suffering for so many years, he is kind and thoughtful and caring towards us, his family, and the people around him. This is not to be taken for granted. Many people who suffer have their worst sides come to the fore – bitterness, anger, jealousy – and family relations are disrupted. I feel very, very lucky and extremely inspired and awed by how he has maintained his generous, loving spirit, even in his lowest of low moments.

Another positive is still having him around. Even though he is not well, he is in my life and part of my life, here to talk to me and give me a hug. Many people don't have fathers in their lives, so having him here with us is a true blessing. I'm grateful for every month and year he is with us.

A weird kind of positive is that the situation has forced my immediate family to come together, to problem-solve, to consider the future and how we will interact in a post-parent world, how we will manage our affairs, what is important to us and what is not. We've had meetings and shared our feelings and ideas. It has put us into a collaborative action phase, which will hopefully prove to be positive in years to come.

Dror

The current personal impact has been the difficulty communicating over the phone, sometimes, and the loss of an active partner in the research program for treating Dov and Lev.

On the positive side, Brian has gained a connectivity with his emotions that was lacking before. It certainly seems that bursts of tears mark moments of joy and sorrow. These are signs of a life more fully felt and experienced. Brian also shines in his tenacity for making the best of things. He is not a victim of Parkinson's, choosing rather to become an advocate for raising awareness about the disease, living with it, and improving treatment through research. I am in awe of how he finds the courage to face his fears and tribulations, and then the energy to create a positive outcome. I also admire Brian's determination to stay focused on family, to keep everyone together and united, bound by loyalty to himself and the values that he has nurtured. I am still constantly learning from him.

Carrie

Brian has emerged as a calm presence, and even in his difficult situation, he retains the ability to see through to the core of things.

Gene

In response to Brian's condition, slowing down and staying in one place have become high priorities for me. Brian may not see to what extent I have reduced my workload. I still devote long hours to SCCI and continue to research and complete priority tasks over weekends. However, by comparison with my much more rushed, peripatetic schedule during the past three decades, Brian now slows me down – a blessing in many ways.

I stay home at night, forgoing most events, functions, openings and dinners – bar evenings when I have agreed to speak, open an exhibition, or when there are exceptional circumstances.

Family members already closely connected with one another have, I feel, drawn even closer. We miss Ondine terribly, but because of Brian's illness she calls more often than she otherwise would have done. Dror's real abiding love for Brian has been so much in evidence. His wise words, 'Quiet voice, loud actions,' resonate with us all.

Despite Brian's suffering and everyday courageous battle – to walk, talk and manage tasks we take for granted – he still manages to attract people to his cause. A business friend, Richard, who has

Parkinson's himself has taken him on as a 'project' despite never having met Brian as a high functioning, high energy, charismatic person. Tomer met Brian in Tel Aviv – unwell and barely coping with his daily routine or Dov and Lev's bar mitzvah events. He too found Brian an inspiration.

In short, Brian's courage, determination and drive – added to his gentle spirit – serve as inspiration for each one of us. Ondine and Dror's lived experience, calm acceptance and deep love for their special-needs boys, echoes the strength, bravery and evolved understanding that Brian has brought and brings to his life.

Finally, his Sydney-based grandsons, who see him regularly, have learnt lessons related to caring and compassion via their interactions with him. A healthy, active grandfather might have played tennis and chess with them. However, observing frailty combined with courage and love for family must surely give them positive messages about living meaningful lives.

Untitled (date unknown)

Ongoing Conflict Continued (2021)

'On the Surface', Watercolour Wash: Brian's *Interpretation of a Freestyle Surfer* (2021)

2020

The previous year ended on a high note. Still, the ebbs and flows of my condition are accompanied by a dark undertow – the knowledge that this journey, in the end, is one way. In early 2020, I notice the acceleration of certain symptoms, some peculiar and mentally troubling, some, I assume, par for the course.

Exhaustion and lethargy are constant. I long to wake up refreshed, but every day feels like a mountain to climb. Profound fatigue now overwhelms me, yet I don't have the urge to sleep, or even rest. My breathing is laboured, and at times my head seems too heavy for my neck to hold up. Not infrequently, I have the sensation of being semi-comatose. There are short stretches where I lose myself and seem to have no thoughts. A blankness takes over my mind, obliterating my short-term memory.

Things improve late at night, watching TV with Gene. The rest of the day is tough and getting tougher. I try to reserve what energy I have for my schedule of appointments and therapy – speech therapy, personal training, drumming, physio, my psychotherapist, art therapy, and so on – and various work commitments, all of which benefit my overall wellbeing.

Nevertheless, I am conscious of my increasing frailty. There is a visceral sense that I am taking a further irreversible step into the abyss. My feeling is that the dopamine is no longer giving me the coverage it once did. For one thing, I notice my right hand has a slight tremor – a symptom I first recognised some eight years ago, before my diagnosis.

My walking, too, has deteriorated further. I miss the freedom of the simple act of getting up and taking a purposeful stride. It is amazing to me now what we take for granted.

2020 is notable as the year I progress from a walking stick to a walking frame. My circumstances are determined by it, and I rely on it more and more. I use it to leverage up off chairs and to make my way from one part of the house to another, or on longer outings. I had the queen bed removed from my room and replaced with a double, so I can manoeuvre the frame around it as I totter to the bathroom at night

Later, a wheelchair is discussed. It is too confronting, and I am not ready to go there yet. Once, I prided myself on my vitality. The decline to decrepitude is a hard pill. I picture my father-in-law, Eric, submerged in the metaphorical jar of honey from which there is no escape. Funnily enough, though, I can still play a reasonable game of table tennis with my grandchildren. Muscle memory and reflexes must be the last to go.

My travails are not merely physical. My dream life now centres on vivid and disturbing imagery of the Holocaust. I retain only fragments, but the dreams are accompanied by a feeling of foreboding. In one, I see a friend's twin daughters in the swimming pool at their home. The sisters are separated, and one is taken away by Nazi guards. In this horror story, we know what happens next.

When awake, I experience something akin to lucid dreaming in the form of visual and tactile hallucinations, and their frequency is increasing. The PD, I assume, is playing havoc with my mind. Everyday objects shape-shift and morph before my eyes, and I see people who are not there. It's as if I dwell in some twilight zone between the realm of the well and a netherworld that exists only for me, the solitary viewer of an obscure experimental film in the theatre of my consciousness. Is it the projection of that ravaged sliver of tissue deep in my brain?

Yet I am not ready to give up. In the company of Gene, Emile and Natalie, I speak with my neurologist about potential new therapies currently being tested in clinical trials, one at the hospital with which he is affiliated, and one with a Parkinson's research foundation. My specialist does not agree that I should embark on either trial. His view is that the negatives – including possible side effects and unknown consequences – far outweigh any potential gains. I feel very disappointed but, for now, accept his opinion.

Alongside all of this, my view on life and death has been changing. The human spirit is always looking to move forward, but now I am confronted daily with the brutal realisation of mortality, and there is not a damn thing I can do about it.

Otherwise, I am perfectly fine.

In fact, despite it all, remarkably, at some very deep level, I detect an infinitesimal turn for the better. There is a subtle shift in my perceptions. Overall, my anxiety is reduced, and with it the turmoil and tumult that had blighted me all these Parkinson's years. In myself, I am more stable. Perhaps I am learning, slowly, gradually, in imperceptible increments, to come to terms with my fate.

MONDAY, 31 AUGUST 2020

11:55am

I'm sitting in the sunroom noticing my hands. Both feel very strange. There is a sensation of 'wooliness', as if I could pull a couple of strands of yarn from my palm.

This has been going on for a few months; it must be a manifestation of the PD. Feels like I am holding a very light tissue all the time. I will ask my doctor when I see him next. Odd.

Sometimes, I have a sensation that my right hand is grasping a spider's web. It stretches between my fingers, sticky and hard to remove. I try to pull it off. It feels so real that when the sensation dissipates, I am convinced that I managed to remove it.

I notice that the shadows of the curtains look like baby monkeys. The other day, I was convinced I saw a tiny bird in the corner of a cardboard box. I asked Natalie or Ron if they saw it, and of course, they didn't, but I felt sure it was there. Later, the flowers on the table took on the appearance of a human head.

A few nights ago, I walked into the house and saw two elderly people who were unknown to me sitting in the TV room.

I retreated from the room, and then went back in. They were still there, just sitting, not saying anything. It was unnerving. I wanted to know what they were doing there, and to get rid of them. It felt so real.

Eventually, to my relief, they melted away, and I was able to go to bed and sleep.

THURSDAY, 3 SEPTEMBER 2020

11:25am

On a bright note, we brought home a new member of the family last weekend, a Maltese poodle. He's sweet and cute and a bit vocal. It's going to take him a while to get used to us all. New home, new people, new smells. His name is Miette, and he will be Gene's dog.

TUESDAY, 20 OCTOBER 2020

Pepper arrived last Friday, my new five-year-old beagle/King Charles spaniel from the RSPCA. He is calm and affectionate, and will be my companion.

While no one can fill the hole left by Miracle, it is good to have a dog again. Dogs have been an integral part of my emotional life since my youth, and the relationships I have with them have been profoundly important to me. I have no doubt Pepper and I will become firm friends.

*　*　*

I decide to see a psychiatrist who specialises in neurofeedback, in which one learns to modulate brain function, guided by feedback from EEG signals. There is some evidence that it helps motor function in PD. This doctor also recommends neurofeedback as a way to improve sleep, which he believes is foundational to health and critical in improving symptom control in Parkinson's.

First, I must travel to his office for a diagnostic QEEG – a Quantitative EEG, also known as brain mapping. For three gruelling hours my head is encased in a gel-filled cap and connected via electrodes to a computer that registers brain waves. I am given headphones and am required to listen for certain sounds and press buttons on a PC when I hear them. It is too much; I do not complete it. Nor do I do the recommended overnight sleep study. It is too complicated and invasive in my diminished state. I determine with Gene that it is not worth proceeding.

A while later, I do give it a try. The machinery is brought to my home. I am hooked up via electrodes to a monitor that flashes red and green all night, and have oxygen tubing inserted in my nostrils. I become disoriented and can't tolerate it, detaching myself from the tubing and wires. That is the end of that.

Another result is pleasing. My prostate cancer blood marker is down again. There will be no repeat of the debilitating radiation treatment I endured in 2018.

MONDAY, 2 NOVEMBER 2020

1:48pm

Taking my pills has become a real chore. My coordination is so poor, I worry I may miss my mouth. Swallowing remains a challenge; I have the uncomfortable sensation that the pills are stuck and I'm choking. I struggle to even bring the pills up to my mouth from my hand.

Same for when I am lying on the floor due to low BP. I must use all my muscle strength to get down and then hoist myself back up. It is such a simple task, yet it exhausts me, and I am not always successful.

Yesterday, I had a fall. Got onto my knees from the lying position on the carpet, tried to stand up, and collapsed to the ground. Luckily, no injury was done.

Today, my feet are terribly swollen – I have them up on a chair. I had a hard time taking my shoes off.

Nevertheless, I had a good weekend. We had some people over for lunch yesterday and I was able to converse and be part of it all. We also had Zachy's thirteenth birthday dinner on Friday night with lots of family, which was lovely.

Natalie is here, and we are having a session with my therapist soon. She struggles to understand me and Natalie translates and updates her on anything new. I am then seeing a new physio who can hopefully help me with my lower back/hip issues.

An old friend was here for an hour and a half for coffee. Was good to see him.

Heading towards the end of a very odd year.

COVID

Lost Miracle

Found Pepper.

FRIDAY, 27 NOVEMBER 2020

12:43pm

Yesterday, Gene and I were featured on the front page of the *Sydney Morning Herald*. We had made a donation to the Australian Museum, where I served as president of the Board of Trustees for nine years. I am humbled by the acknowledgement. The museum has gone through a major refurbishment, and a hall is to be dedicated in my name at a ceremony in December.

To my great delight, Ondine is in Sydney, but in hotel quarantine for one more week due to COVID. It feels strange to have her so close, but not yet be able to see her. Not long now. She will join us at the Australian Museum event.

WEDNESDAY, 16 DECEMBER 2020

I am at the Brian Sherman Crystal Hall dedication dinner at the Australian Museum. It is a magnificent sandstone edifice dating from the 19th Century, and a revered scientific, cultural and research institution. My association goes back twenty years, to when I commenced my term as president of the Museum Trust.

Guest numbers are capped at 60 due to COVID. Family, good friends, senior staff and state politicians, as well as museum trustees, have come to celebrate with me.

I enter shakily on Gene's arm, with my children, Emile and Ondine, by our sides. My daughter-in-law Carrie and grandchildren Zachary, Milo and Cy round out the family contingent. I miss Jasmine, Dror and the twins, who remain in Israel, but feel blessed to have the others here with me on a special night.

At the entrance to the hall is a brass plaque bearing my name. I stand by it, as the guests are ushered in and photographed with me in turn. Inside the imposing space, a beautiful, intimate dinner setting has been created with ten large round tables, a stage and a main screen at the back.

Gene gives a speech as a collage of images from my life plays behind her: photos of me as a boy, my family, my dogs and my days at the museum. It is very emotional. Next, the museum director and a senior politician say a few words. Lastly, it is my turn. I had hesitated at the thought of public speaking, as I struggle to be heard and understood – my voice is weak, and I tend now to stutter or gasp for breath, especially as my anxiety mounts. The solution was to film a five-minute video of my speech at home. It plays on the screen, and, to my mind, surpasses all the speeches I gave over the years of my business life, including the many I delivered in my role at the museum.

To conclude proceedings, my cousin Lloyd's wife, Joanna, a highly accomplished musician and vocalist, sings a song – 'The Artists are Leaving' – accompanied by an exquisite violin solo.

Everything is perfect.

***

Revisiting my time at the helm of the museum, surrounded by my family, close friends and colleagues, gives me pause to reflect. I think about my life thus far, and my Parkinson's journey.

I've been in my predicament, at the mercy of PD, for ten years now. As I have detailed in this account, its reach extends to every aspect of my being. A decade on, the brute fact is that despite extensive medical research into Parkinson's, there is no sign of the cavalry riding in at the last minute to save me. I remain open to new therapeutic possibilities, however I am realistic about the prospects for treatment, which will likely be limited to symptom control at best. A cure remains stubbornly elusive.

My hope is that for fellow sufferers in the future, it will be a different story – one with an unequivocally happy ending, where some potion or pill, some combination of drugs or zap to the brain, banishes this cruel affliction, or, even better, prevents it altogether. For myself, each day is *déjà vu*, and decline is inevitable. The path ahead is hard and will only get harder as I am beset with increasing infirmity.

I am sure I'm not alone amongst those living with chronic, degenerative or terminal illnesses in asking, Why? Of course, I can't speak for anyone but myself on this conundrum. My own feeling is that the traumas I suffered in my younger life may have played a part – my mother-in-law's suicide when Gene and I were newlyweds, and the full-term stillbirth of Gene's and my first child among them. Nor do I underestimate the legacy of the Holocaust written into my genes, or my formative years as witness to the atrocities of Apartheid. My exposure to the unfathomable abuse we inflict daily on billions of sentient food animals is inscribed deep in my psyche, a wound that will not heal. On a physical level, the gruelling eighteen-hour days on the road with my business, EquitiLink, plagued by insomnia and soldiering on through various everyday illnesses, could not have helped but take a toll.

I am not completely out on a limb here. I have come across research that suggests stress, grief and trauma may trigger an underlying predisposition to neurodegenerative illnesses such as Parkinson's, or make the dopamine-producing cells vulnerable to the impacts of further stress.

The precipitating events may be deep in the past, or closer in time to the onset of the condition. I know in my case, there were late-life traumas, too. My obsessive quest over many years to 'fix' the twins was one. It took me some time to arrive at the epiphany that the brokenness was not in Dov and Lev, but in the lens through which I viewed them.

Whatever the case, it is common knowledge that mind and body are inseparably enmeshed, and that emotional distress has a profound impact on our physical being. Then again, all of us bear our crosses, some more weighty than mine, and not all are struck down with a debilitating affliction. No one-to-one correspondence between cause and effect, trauma and disease, can be found. If the truth be known, when confronted with a devastating diagnosis, one could equally ask, Why *not*? We all have our Waterloos. The question of the origin of my Parkinson's must remain open in the end, a definitive answer unattainable in my lifetime.

What is clear is this: I am a fortunate human being. I have known – still know – great love. Family has been my bedrock, three-quarters of a century ago in the stable home in Brakpan where I grew up, and now. I have my beloved wife, two children, six grandchildren and extended family, and it is one of my life's blessings that we are close. In business, I've won some battles and lost others, but that is par for the course. My professional success – in no small part due to good luck as well as ingenuity and hard work – has given me opportunities beyond my wildest imaginings to do things in the world, through my philanthropy and other work. When I reflect on my epitaph, I imagine the words, 'I saw, and I acted.'

As the dusk of my lifetime falls, there is a sense of pride and satisfaction in what I have achieved, and gratitude for my lot in life.

I know, also, that I am not alone in my plight. It is the human condition. Very few of us have the exceptional luck to slip away peacefully in our sleep at a grand age, free of illness, or be transported in an instant, unwittingly, to the afterlife. For most, there is existential pain and loss at the end, whether one's demise is long and drawn out or mercifully short.

For my part, I have my reasonable days and my bad days – or rather, the fluctuations of my symptoms, mental and physical, are measured in minutes or hours. Compared to the beginning of my journey, I find myself on calmer seas. Perhaps I have surrendered some of the doggedness that drove me for so many years in my personal and professional life, at times to my detriment. Maybe I have finally been granted a little of the serenity I need to begin to accept this thing that I cannot change. The struggle continues – and it is tough – but there is also, at least in part, a settling into my situation, and with it, the tentative lifting of a burden.

At the end of the long evening, it is time to depart. I am touched by the generous and warm farewells from the guests. Supported by Gene, I make my painstaking exit from the darkened entrance to the museum, doing the slow Parkinson's shuffle. The weather is pleasantly mild and the air, still and quiet. I am heading back to my happy, loving home a short drive away. As is to be expected after an evening out, I am utterly spent.

But for just a brief moment here or there, on this night, I forget the earthly shackles of my disease, and have wings.

Brian Sherman's music therapy (Brian playing drums at home), multiple exposure composite photograph by Gary Grealy

Ongoing Conflict (2021)

Meshed In (2021)

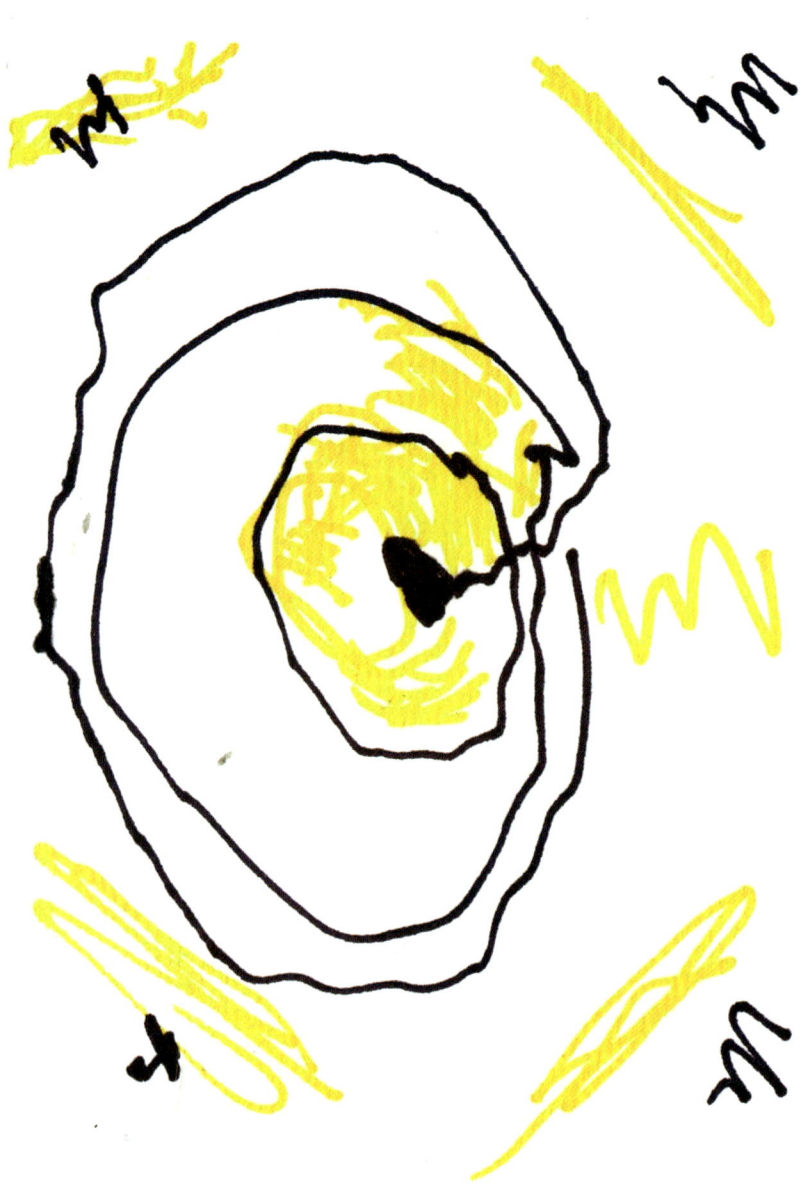

Abstract in Yellow and Purple (2021)

A Medical Perspective

Dr Stephen Tisch, Neurologist

My neurologist, Dr Stephen Tisch, has been working with me since 2017. I asked him to offer some insights that I hope will be useful for readers, and so, in the following interview, Stephen talks with AM Jonson about Parkinson's disease from his professional perspective.

AM JONSON: How has Brian fared from when you first met him to now? How did he originally present, how has he progressed, and what is the expected course of his illness?

DR S TISCH: When Brian presented, he was experiencing recognised symptoms of Parkinson's disease, including slowness, stiffness, restricted movement. Little bit of tremor. He was also experiencing a lot of dizziness. A lot of anxiety. And that overshadowed some of the motor symptoms, making the diagnosis a bit tricky. But I was fairly convinced that he met the criteria for Parkinson's disease and moved forward in that direction, in a more concerted way to try and address those symptoms. That worked quite well, and although his disease has definitely progressed, his overall progression has been gentler than perhaps one might have expected when we started the journey.

I have treated Brian very carefully and used the full range of treatments, including some more advanced treatments like his medication infusion pump. But I think a lot of it is down to him, taking stock and taking action on his part, to mitigate the impacts of the disease. For example, Brian has fully embraced exercise and physiotherapy. He does a range of other activities that help his mobility and balance. He plays ping pong regularly. Does stretching. He goes for walks. And he remains very socially engaged, which is a hugely important way of maintaining communication and cognition.

He's cut down his calendar a little, but he still does a lot of things in the community and his family.

I think all of these activities that he has undertaken, which I've strongly encouraged, have very much mitigated the impacts of the disease over time. I think he has arrived at a point that is arguably better than he would have been had he not done these things.

I think he sees that as well, and I think he is reasonably happy with the way his Parkinson's disease has been managed, and what I've done for him and what he has done for himself.

AMJ: Yes, I think he is very happy considering how he was a few years ago. Seems to have somewhat stabilised and be doing well.

DR S TISCH: Stabilised, exactly, and we are still trying to break ground with treatment,

We're taking some more active steps using medication to actually try and slow the disease down if we can – using at times an innovative and still exploratory approach. At the moment there is no definitive therapy that can achieve the objectives we had in mind. There are, however, a number of compounds and medicines that seem to show potential. Brian's enthusiasm to take on challenges allows me to pull out all stops in terms of his treatment.

He is very engaged. He is very, very clear with respect to making decisions about his treatment. I give him advice about what to do, but ultimately he remains the decision maker. He's actually very, very easy to treat in that regard. We get on extremely well.

AMJ: Drawing on your expertise, what is known about the causes of PD and what is the incidence in the community? And is it growing?

DR S TISCH: It is estimated that up to two to three per cent of the population will be impacted by Parkinson's at some point in their lives. It is becoming a more prevalent and a significant problem.

In the last 30 years, there has been a definite increase worldwide and the reasons for that are not fully understood. They're not completely explained by us living longer or the ageing population, although it is fair to say that increases in the onset of symptoms have been particularly noticeable in people over the age of 70.

The cause of Parkinson's is still not understood at an individual level, so I can't give people a straight answer when they ask me what has caused their Parkinson's. But we do know that there are various things that are thought to be risk factors for developing PD, including living in a rural environment. Exposure to certain pesticides seems to increase the lifetime risk. Curiously, there is some added risk for lifelong non-smokers. Active or passive smoking has some protective effects in Parkinson's. This is interesting and a bit unexpected.

Also, we know that there is some genetic contribution to the cause of Parkinson's. The risks tend to increase in patients with multiple affected family members – although, conventionally, it is generally not considered a genetic disorder. It is rare that it will run in families and be attributable to a specific gene. Those patients do exist, but they experience the relatively rare, so-called genetic forms of Parkinson's. To our knowledge, Brian isn't in that category.

I think that at a community level and as an issue for modern societies, Parkinson's is a growing problem. The number of people with Parkinson's disease is increasing, and with it are all the burdens the disease places, not only on the patient, but also on their families and community, and the costs to the healthcare system as well.

AMJ: Going to that point of managing the disease burden, what are the most effective treatments or approaches to management of PD currently, and what kinds of new or innovative treatments are coming down the line?

DR S TISCH: At this stage, we don't have definitive disease modifying or curative treatment. The emphasis is on early correct diagnosis and, where appropriate, early symptomatic treatment, usually in the form of medications that increase dopamine levels in the brain. The gold standard medication remains a drug called levodopa, which is still among the most widely prescribed. Brian receives this particular medication. It was discovered for clinical use in Parkinson's in the late 1960s and has remained a cornerstone of treatment for Parkinson's ever since.

Levodopa, in combination with other drugs that act on the dopamine system, as well as a range of other medications, can significantly reduce the symptoms, particularly motor symptoms, and improve motor function, the ability of patients to remain active, and the quality of life and rate of survival.

Medication is only one part of the treatment. Patients also require physical therapy and these days we strongly advocate Parkinson's specific exercise and physiotherapy, which has a strong evidence base. There is quite a lot of literature supporting the superiority of these types of exercise programs over generic exercise. Typically, these exercise programs emphasise large-scale movement with lots of novelty. When patients are learning new movement patterns on a large whole-body scale with lots of vigour, energy and encouragement, this seems to open up output channels within the motor system to encourage a favourable plastic response in the brain, so that patients can relearn some motor skills that might have been lost.

They improve automation as well as the strength and fitness that goes along with it. These exercise therapies have a very definite and remarkable benefit to patients with Parkinson's disease. It is now considered crucial that anyone with Parkinson's, including early diagnosed patients, is told about these programs and then receives this type of exercise therapy in conjunction with optimised medication. That combined approach has delivered significantly greater benefits than using medication alone.

In terms of other treatments, as the disease progresses, patients frequently develop unstable responses to levodopa. For example, patients may have a distinct phase of improvement after taking their levodopa medication, but it might only last a few hours. Then that improvement will decay and leave them in a state of poorer function with return of difficult symptoms, such as slowness, stiffness, walking difficulties, tremor, for example. That pattern of unstable motor responses, with phases of improvement as well as phases of deterioration corresponding to the timing of medication intake, we call motor fluctuation on/off periods, as well as dyskinesias, involuntary jerky movements.

These problems accrue overtime. Most people after five to ten years of levodopa treatment will be experiencing something of this sort to varying degrees, and indeed Brian was experiencing these problems.

Together we instituted a more advanced therapy, one of the device-assisted therapies, which is something called an apomorphine infusion. It was developed in the 1980s, and I have quite a lot of familiarity with this therapy.

I suggested that we use this method of treatment when Brian's symptoms were starting to become increasingly unstable with oral medications alone, three or four years ago now. And that has been an excellent benefit for Brian in stabilising his motor fluctuations. It has really improved his quality of life, and it's something that he continues to use and derive substantial benefit from.

This is just one example of a more innovative therapy that can help solve problems as they appear. We can also deliver continuous medication infusions (Levodopa Carbidopa intestinal gel infusion, the proprietary name is Dua-Dopa) in the form of levodopa injected directly into the small bowel. Brian hasn't tried this yet, but it is certainly a good option for patients.

We also have a neuromodulation in the form of deep brain stimulation (DBS), which is the implantation of electrodes into the brain, powered by a small, implanted pacemaker, an entirely internalised system. This DBS approach also can provide substantial relief of motor fluctuation, tremor, dyskinesia, and greatly improve a patient's quality of life, usually for patients with moderately advanced symptoms.

That is an overview of currently available therapies.

AMJ: In terms of newer therapies coming down the line, are there any other prospects?

DR S TISCH: In the newer therapies we're actively looking for disease-modifying treatments in PD.

I'm involved in a national multicentre study looking at this exact issue called the Australian Parkinson's Mission. We are one of six sites nationally exploring three particular medications compared to a placebo, to see whether any of these medications have the potential to stabilise or reverse the impacts of the disease at the level of disease modification.

For something to be disease modifying, not only is it treating the symptoms, it is actually slowing down the biological processes within the brain, or even potentially reversing the underlying pathological changes in the brain – a very exciting option because it holds the promise of slowing the disease down, or even pausing the progression of the disease, which is something patients are very keen to obtain.

At this stage, those approaches are still exploratory and there is no proven therapy, but it is certainly something we are very keen to try and develop.

And as I mentioned, Brian has recently started a different medication that has putative neuro-protective properties. I'm going to continue to monitor him in response to that medication, to see if it can favourably impact his disease progression.

AMJ: Do you believe a cure is possible and in what sort of timeframe?

DR S TISCH: I would love to believe there is a cure possible and I think eventually there will be one, but I think it will come very incrementally – probably from a series of unexpected discoveries, like so many things in medicine. There is often an element of luck and serendipity for major breakthroughs.

Probably within my lifetime we will have the first-generation disease modifying drugs, which show unequivocal disease stabilisation. In Parkinson's disease it might not be just a single drug, possibly a cocktail: two, three or four drugs all targeting different convergent pathways that contribute to Parkinson's disease, a multi-drug approach. We might also end up targeting genes which are overexpressed in Parkinson's disease. So rather than targeting the enzymes and chemical pathways directly, we could target gene expression – that might be another future focus for Parkinson's disease researchers.

There are many groups worldwide that are actively looking at these various approaches, so I think it's conceivable that within the next 20 or 30 years we will have the first generation of disease-modifying medications that might not reverse Parkinson's disease but, at the very least, demonstrably delay its progression.

I think that is the first step. If we could slow the disease down even by fifteen to twenty per cent, that would make a big difference for patients. It would mean they would have a gentler disease course, and to an extent some of the long-term impacts would be neutralised. If patients' overall disease burden is milder at the point at which they reach old age, in some way the threat of the disease will have been neutralised, even if we can't cure it all together.

This is my very firm hope. I think it is achievable. I think it is realistic within the timeframe of perhaps the next one, two or three decades. I'm very keen to contribute to this work, and I'm involved in studies which try to make first steps towards finding medications that will achieve meaningful goals.

AMJ: In the meantime, is there anything that people can do to protect their brain health and reduce their risk?

DR S TISCH: We wouldn't recommend taking up smoking. Although statistically at the moment, that probably would be one of the most effective ways of reducing your risk of Parkinson's. The health detriment would overall outweigh that benefit.

It is generally felt that we need to try and lead active lifestyles throughout life and continue to exercise at all points in our lives; to minimise our intake of toxins, including alcohol, but also avoid as much as possible exposure to environmental chemicals including, if we can, avoiding highly processed foods. We should all be gravitating to varied foods, of unprocessed origins – be they organic or non-organic. At the very least, we should eat well. Food should be as unprocessed as possible, and we should avoid foods with e-numbers in the list of ingredients.

Patients should pay attention to their sleep quality. They should make sure that they get enough sleep and avoid sleep deprivation and exhaustion. I think there is emerging evidence that chronic sleep deprivation or poor sleep could either be a marker or a risk factor for neurodegeneration. Sleep is certainly a great healer, even for people with established neurodegenerative diseases or Parkinson's disease, and improving sleep quality could often have beneficial effects on the person's condition.

People should maintain strong social networks and personal relationships and remain connected at a social level, engaging in regular, robust discourse with their peers. The old-fashioned way, meeting at a café or restaurant and having robust discussions with friends. This remains probably one of the best forms of cognitive training one can do. It is true when you're 30, 40, 50, 60 or 70-plus, because it keeps you on your toes. You have to formulate your ideas in order to articulate what it is you want to say, and so it is testing all of the things that the brain was designed to do.

This is certainly the message I give my patients – that if you sit in the corner doing crosswords or sudoku, you will be exercising part of your brain, but a very small part. What is needed is integrated real-world activities, such as robust conversations in a group.

I try to apply these principles personally and I think everyone can do that. I believe that we have arrived at a heightened awareness of health, generally speaking. I do feel that society is moving away from health-damaging activities to some extent. We're seeing the rates of smoking decline, we're seeing reduction in alcohol consumption, typically amongst younger people. There are many people taking exercise seriously and with healthy diet awareness. I think these new behaviours will help.

Whether all of this translates into a reduction in the future prevalence of Parkinson's disease remains to be seen. Parkinson's numbers are climbing – for reasons that we don't fully understand.

AMJ: So interesting, an holistic approach to maintaining health. Going back to Brian, what is his outlook from here?

DR S TISCH: Brian knows that he is in the grip of a neurodegenerative condition.

We've had some hard talks where he said, 'What does the late stage look like?' And I said that looking at very late stage people, they have great difficulty walking and may have great difficulty swallowing. Their cognition will often be more impaired and may fluctuate. They may have periods of lucidity as well as periods of confusion. They may have problems with continence.

They may be at risk of falls if they do mobilise. There will be a number of high-risk eventualities that could ensue in that late stage, including choking when attempting to eat, resulting in aspiration pneumonia, or a fall resulting in fracture, or a really serious infection due to a urinary tract infection.

It is fair to say that the path of late stage Parkinson's disease is paved with hazards. Some patients with Parkinson's die of completely unrelated causes, but some of my patients do, in a sense, die of their Parkinson's. That is because the impacts of the disease put them at great risk for one of these late stage complications. That is a very confronting thing to think about. Brian is very knowledgeable, he has done a lot of personal research, and I've certainly been up front with him when he has asked me direct questions. He knows that the disease is a progressive one.

There will come a time when he has significantly less function than he does now. While we both work very hard to stave off the impacts of the disease, there has been some decline. There was significant stabilisation after apomorphine was introduced. But even since then, I think there has been some downward decline year by year, which he would admit to. It reflects the tempo of disease progression.

At the moment, we're relatively powerless to stop that. We just have to accept it. This is one of the reasons Brian was highly motivated to try an exploratory medication as putative neuroprotection, and I supported him in that decision. We'll see how that goes. If that delivers disease stabilisation, then we will have really achieved something very, very important.

AMJ: Is Brian a candidate for DBS – deep brain stimulation?

DR S TISCH: I looked at that very carefully. I specialise in this, and I concluded that it would do more harm than good.

I took a 360-degree view forming that impression. It is not just about whether he had severe motor fluctuations. To that end, I think things could improve with DBS to a similar degree as they have with apomorphine. One of the difficulties is that Brian's cognition, although strong in certain areas, has been showing fragility now for a number of years. One of my major concerns was that there would be a very real risk of his cognition, formidable cognition, really decompensating after a major brain surgery like deep brain stimulation. I thought, given that he lives through his mind in many ways, anything that stood to jeopardise that would be a major step back for him, and probably overshadow any benefits associated with motor improvement.

My feeling was that we avoid deep brain stimulation. I think the longer we've gone on, Brian has been very happy with that advice. He was not at all keen on the idea either. Certainly some of the other senior neurologists who have been involved in his management, including those in Israel, have pretty much endorsed the path we've taken.

AMJ: Brian has a plant-based diet, as you know, and you did mention diet as part of the holistic approach to management.

DR S TISCH: I think his diet been really good for him in that it has tackled a couple of the indirect issues relating to Parkinson's. For example, constipation hasn't been much of a problem for Brian, perhaps because of these plant-based foods.

Sometimes dietary protein can also negate some of the effectiveness of some of the drugs that we use to treat Parkinson's. Brian's intake of dietary protein has been gentler and more evenly distributed, because of his plant-based diet.

Also, if people are consuming plant-based diets, they are much less likely to be consuming highly processed foods. Even in people who are more omnivorous and consuming animal products as well, using source ingredients to prepare your food and avoiding packets and processed products is a very good tip, and Brian's been doing that implicitly with his plant-based diet.

AMJ: Terrific, I think that covers what we had hoped to achieve. Thank you. That's incredibly comprehensive and helpful. Is there anything else that you'd like to add?

DR S TISCH: I'd just add that Brian has great personal qualities. I know he's a rather special guy, the community at large views him as a special and generous person and he has achieved a lot.

Also, I think he's a very, very personable, gentle, lovely person who has also been incredibly resilient, so he's been a real pleasure to manage. We've always got on well, and although he's a well-known person, he's very humble, doesn't stand on pretense or ceremony, so it's been a very positive experience treating him and his family, and those comments extend to Gene and the family at large.

I feel fortunate that I have him as a patient. He's a great guy.

You know, I'm looking forward to continuing to treat him, whatever comes. I think we're in this for the long haul. Brian and I have formed a bond, and I envisage we will continue to work together from now on.

Dr Stephen Tisch MBBS (Hons) PhD FRACP
Consultant Neurologist
Staff Specialist in Neurology
Head of Department, Neurology
Conjoint Associate Professor UNSW
Adjunct Associate Professor University of Notre Dame

Joy (2021)

Reflective Painting of Bondi Beach (2021)

Brian Sherman's speech therapy, multiple exposure
composite photograph by Gary Grealy

Green Tangle (2021)

Walking Through Honey – The Video Series

Rod Freedman

As both Gene Sherman's cousin and a documentary filmmaker, I enthusiastically embraced Gene's suggestion of recording aspects of Brian's life with Parkinson's disease on film. Given that *Walking Through Honey* is almost entirely written from his own perspective, I decided to focus on Brian's experience with three of the therapies that are now an important part of his life – exercise, speech and art.

Working with his therapists, Brian and I explored his experiences relating to movement, communication and artistic expression. Together we looked at the attempts Brian and the therapists make to slow down the debilitating effects of the disease, and investigated why these activities are helpful for him.

The videos aim to give Brian a voice, so viewers can understand what he is experiencing, physically and emotionally. Our goals became increasingly important as his speech and capacity for communication noticeably declined in the months prior to filming.

Over a period of time, we had a series of one-on-one conversations in Brian's quiet study at home – a place where he feels most relaxed. These exchanges form the core of the videos.

At times, Brian found talking arduous. He has his on and off days. The intensity of his symptoms varies during the day, as his medications kick in and then wear off. Sometimes we'd pause during the filming because he couldn't articulate his thoughts, the right words eluding him. However, he tenaciously persisted, sharing his struggle with his 'invisible enemy'.

'You're living with a disease that's eroding your soul. Your whole being is under attack. You're going backwards when you've always gone forward, so your progress is reversed,' Brian says.

The videos complement this book as you're able to 'meet' Brian and hear his own words, while seeing the effort he puts in with regard to his various activities. He makes no attempt to be falsely positive: 'You don't grow with Parkinson's, it is simply a battle to defend yourself.'

I learnt to ask questions and then wait patiently while Brian formed his thoughts. Normally, one would find such silences uncomfortable, and jump in to fill spaces, robbing the other person of the chance to get started and build up to speed. Likening his communication efforts to driving a car, Brian describes his forced move from 'automatic', to a more deliberate 'manual' process.

Brian's life experiences have ricocheted from huge highs through to abysmal lows. He has gone from high-profile community recognition to personal challenges and family tragedies. In the 1980s and '90s, he achieved extraordinary financial success through Equitlink, the fund management company he co-founded with my brother, Laurence Freedman. He successfully chaired the Finance Committee for the 2000 Sydney Olympic Games. He is acknowledged as one of Sydney's leading philanthropists and has dedicated himself to an ethical and compassionate stance in life. This is exemplified by Voiceless, the animal protection and advocacy organisation he founded in 2004 with his daughter, Ondine.

In the videos, we meet Brian at a time when Parkinson's has transformed his life. They capture a person struggling with the decline of those capabilities that brought him fortune and renown. 'There is no bright side, there is no light at the end of the tunnel, it's a road downhill.'

Yet, Brian remains recognisable in his essence – a deeply sensitive man in touch with his emotions, willing and determined to explore and express his feelings. He generously shares his circumstances, hopeful that openness and honesty will help others understand the myriad aspects of living with this cruel disease.

Writing *Walking Through Honey* and participating in the associated videos have clearly helped him. 'I found it a positive experience, finding out about myself. It gave me something to work on, to assist me in understanding what life's all about.'

As a tightly knit close family, the Freedmans, Shermans and other family clusters often gather in large groups, punctuated by multiple, overlapping conversations. These occasions are mostly joyous and celebratory; the darker, more intimate aspects of our lives are often left relatively unexplored. My sessions filming with Brian have been precious; giving us time together, away from the crowd, seeing eye to eye. The process allowed me to ask direct and often confronting questions, which I would have felt uncomfortable exploring outside of an intimate setting.

I believe the videos reflect that closeness.

I thank Brian for his commitment and honesty, for sharing his pain and his hopes. Living through the most challenging time of his life, he could have been excused for retreating into a shrinking, private world. And yet, the book and the videos show a man determined to reveal himself and, in the process, to help others.

Together, we made three fifteen-minute videos:

Small Steps – Exercise therapy
Shallow Breaths – Speech therapy
Emotion on Paper – Art therapy

You can also view the video of Brian's speech for the Brian Sherman Crystal Hall dedication dinner at the Australian Museum (Wednesday, 16 December 2020).

Briansherman.com.au/videos

Playing Outdoors (2021)

Fragmented Light at the End of the Tunnel (2021)

'Danger Under the Bridge', Watercolour Wash:
Brian's Interpretation of what Lies Beneath the
Harbour (2021)

Artworks by Brian Sherman
Photography by Gary Grealy

Page

i   Brian Sherman, multiple exposure composite portrait © Gary Grealy (2021)

iv–v Brian Sherman's movement therapy (Brian playing table tennis at home), multiple exposure composite photograph © Gary Grealy (2021)

x   *'I Am and Always Be Brian Sherman': Self Portrait of Brian with Miracle*, pastel and crayon on paper, 28.5 × 21.5 centimetres (03.08.2020) © Brian Sherman

xi   *Miracle at Home*, gouache, crayon and plasticine on card, 29.5 × 20.5 centimetres (02.09.2020) © Brian Sherman

xiv *'Hen': A Diptych* (detail), crayon, pastel and gouache on card, 29.6 × 21 centimetres and 40.6 × 29.6 centimetres (04.10.2021) © Brian Sherman

xx   *Heart of the Sea Urchin*, pastel and crayon on paper, 30.5 × 22.8 centimetres (20.01.2021) © Brian Sherman

2   *A Heavy Heart, Being Lightened with Sunshine, Birds and Forest Green,* gouache, pastel, crayon, watercolour and plasticine on card, 42 × 29 centimetres (30.09.2020) © Brian Sherman

5   *Heavy Heart Carrying the Weight of a Whale!,* crayon, pastel watercolour and felt-tip pen on card, 42 × 29.5 centimetres (04.11.2020) © Brian Sherman

6   *'Have a Nice Day!': Message Communicated with Identified Images of Tortoises Making their Way Across the Page*, acrylic and crayon on card, 29.5 × 21 centimetres (23.12.2020) © Brian Sherman

14–15 Brian Sherman's movement therapy (Brian cycling on a stationary bike), multiple exposure composite photograph © Gary Grealy (2021)

20   *Abstract Freedom with Dominant Black*, acrylic and gouache on card, 29.6 × 21 centimetres (13.01.2021) © Brian Sherman

21   *The Appearance of an Image of a Lion: Representative of the Strength of Dealing with the Difficulty of Shallow Breathing*, gouache, felt-tip pen and ink on card, 42 × 29.8 centimetres (09.12.2020) © Brian Sherman

22	*Fragments of Time*, gouache on card, 29.6 × 20.5 centimetres (11.08.2020) © Brian Sherman
34	*Mood Changes I: 'Joy in Colour',* watercolour, crayon, pastel, felt-tip pen and graphite on card, 42 × 29.6 centimetres (08.09.2021) © Brian Sherman
35	*Activity*, gouache on card, 41.9 × 29.6 centimetres (13.09.2021) © Brian Sherman
36	*Yellow Mustard in a Sea of Blue*, gouache on card, 29.7 × 21.6 centimetres (13.01.2021) © Brian Sherman
48	*Abstract Mark-Making:...Identified Dog Image Adding Joy to Otherwise Difficult Day*, watercolour and gouache on card, 41.5 × 29.4 centimetres (14.12.2020) © Brian Sherman
49	*Waking Up*, watercolour on card, 29.6 × 21.7 centimetres (11.08.2021) © Brian Sherman
50	*'Watching in Colour': Emotional Release*, pastel and gouache on card, 41.8 × 29.8 centimetres (28.04.2021) © Brian Sherman
60–61	Brian Sherman's movement and speech therapy (Brian completing a circuit of neck and shoulder muscles stretching), multiple exposure composite photograph © Gary Grealy (2021)
64	*'Softly, Softly', Reflecting on Feeling of Comfort when Resting with Dog – Pepper*, pastel and watercolour on card, 20.6 × 14.8 centimetres (14.04.2021) © Brian Sherman
65	*'Laying Around', Brian's Reflection on the Softness Felt when Spending Quiet Time with Pepper*, pastel and watercolour on card, 29.7 × 28 centimetres (21.09.2021) © Brian Sherman
66	*Freehand Abstract Colour Fill*, pastel, crayon and graphite on paper, 42 × 28 centimetres (06.01.2021) © Brian Sherman
76	*'Books, Books, Books!': Brian's Reflection on Gene's Academia*, pastel, crayon, felt-tip pen and collage on paper, 42 × 29.4 centimetres (19.03.2021) © Brian Sherman
77	*Drawing...On Darkness*, pastel and crayon on card, 41.7 × 29.7 centimetres (16.06.2021) © Brian Sherman
78	*Ondine's Compassionate Heart*, pastel on card, 11.5 × 7.8 centimetres (23.12.2020) © Brian Sherman
88–89	Brian Sherman's movement therapy (Brian walking at a slow and medium pace – in profile), multiple exposure composite photograph © Gary Grealy (2021)
90	*'Hen': A Diptych* (detail), crayon, pastel and gouache on card, 29.6 × 21 centimetres and 40.6 × 29.6 centimetres (04.10.2021) © Brian Sherman
61	*Abstract with Image of a Horse*, pastel, graphite and gouache on card, 41.8 × 29.7 centimetres (26.03.2021) © Brian Sherman
92	*'Beauty Entangled': Brian's Abstract of a Beautiful Girl*, pastel and watercolour on paper, 22.7 × 15.4 centimetres (23.06.2021) © Brian Sherman
102	*Timeless*, gouache and pastel on card, 42 × 29.7 centimetres (25.08.2021) © Brian Sherman
103	*Circle of Time*, gouache and pastel on card, 42 × 29.7 centimetres (01.09.2021) © Brian Sherman
104	*Mood Changes II: 'Willy, Willy',* watercolour on card, 29.6 × 20.7 centimetres (08.09.2021) © Brian Sherman
116	*Unholy Mess*, pastel, crayon, gouache and felt-tip pen on paper, 41.9 × 29.4 centimetres (06.09.2021) © Brian Sherman

ARTWORKS BY BRIAN SHERMAN, PHOTOGRAPHY BY GARY GREALY

117 *Untitled ('Timeless')*, pastel, felt-tip pen and collage on card, 29.6 × 21 centimetres (06.09.2021) © Brian Sherman

118 *Flying Low*, watercolour, felt-tip pen and graphite on card, 21 × 14.9 centimetres (30.07.2021) © Brian Sherman

124–125 Brian Sherman's movement therapy (Brian walking at a slow and medium pace with weights – in profile), multiple exposure composite photograph © Gary Grealy (2021)

130 *Abstract Man and His Dog*, pastel, crayon and gouache on card, 29.6 × 21.1 centimetres (27.02.2021) © Brian Sherman

131 *A Day at the Dentist*, pastel, crayon and watercolour on card, 42 × 29.6 centimetres (17.03.2021) © Brian Sherman

136 *Untitled*, gouache on card, 40.8 × 29.7 centimetres (date unknown) © Brian Sherman

137 *Ongoing Conflict Continued*, gouache on card, 40.9 × 29.7 centimetres (22.09.2021) © Brian Sherman

138 *'On the Surface', Watercolour Wash: Brian's Interpretation of a Freestyle Surfer*, watercolour and pastel on card, 29.6 × 21 centimetres (23.06.2021) © Brian Sherman

150–151 Brian Sherman's music therapy (Brian playing drums at home), multiple exposure composite photograph © Gary Grealy (2021)

152 *Ongoing Conflict*, gouache, pastel and felt-tip pen on card, 42 × 29.6 centimetres (13.09.2021) © Brian Sherman

153 *Meshed In*, gouache on card, 23.6 × 21 centimetres (11.10.2021) © Brian Sherman

154 *Abstract in Yellow and Purple*, felt-tip pen on card, 15 × 10.6 centimetres (23.06.2021) © Brian Sherman

166 *Joy*, gouache on card, 15.1 × 10.4 centimetres (11.10.2021) © Brian Sherman

167 *Reflective Painting of Bondi Beach*, pastel, gouache, felt-tip and sand collected along Bondi Beach on card, 40.1 × 29.6 centimetres (27.10.2021) © Brian Sherman

168–169 Brian Sherman's speech therapy, multiple exposure composite photograph © Gary Grealy (2021)

170 *Green Tangle*, pastel on black paper, 21.1 × 13.8 centimetres (07.04.2021) © Brian Sherman

174 *Playing Outdoors*, crayon and pastel on card, 29.6 × 20.8 centimetres (27.10.2021) © Brian Sherman

175 *Fragmented Light at the End of the Tunnel*, gouache on card, 40.8 × 29.8 centimetres (29.10.2021) © Brian Sherman

176 *'Danger Under the Bridge', Watercolour Wash: Brian's Interpretation of what Lies Beneath the Harbour*, watercolour on card, 29.6 × 21 centimetres (23.06.2021) © Brian Sherman

180 *Woozy Into Black*, pastel and watercolour on paper, 30.4 × 22.9 centimetres (08.04.2021) © Brian Sherman

Woozy Into Black (2021)

Acknowledgements

How to appropriately acknowledge the many wonderful and supportive people who have been part of my Parkinson's journey, both in relation to this book and to the journey itself? I have been fulsomely and caringly assisted and supported in myriad ways, physically, emotionally and spiritually.

First and foremost, I extend my heartfelt thanks to my core book team: to co-writer AM Jonson, whose consummate skills deftly helped weave the threads of my experience into the fluent and lyrical narrative you read here, building on the work she did in my memoir, *The Lives of Brian*; to Natalie Lotkin, my Executive Assistant and Sherman Group Human Resources Manager, who has worked by my side for seventeen years, a trained psychotherapist and my daily sounding board and support – perceptive, smart and intuitive – and the sensitive translator of my thoughts for the diary notes that helped form part of this book; and to Barry Sechos, my right-hand man at The Sherman Group, whose constant support on all levels is very much appreciated.

My warmest thanks go to Jeffrey Masson, my dear friend, for his generous and insightful foreword; to award-winning documentary director and producer, Rod Freedman, for his outstanding work on the video component of this project, and to brilliant photographer, Gary Grealy, whose fine eye captured the evocative images you see within these pages.

To publisher Jon MacDonald, editor Bernadette Foley, designer Daniel New, and SCCI Head of Marketing and Communications David Congram, I thank each of you for your commitment to this publication and your steady and expert stewardship in bringing the book to fruition.

My journey has been, in large part, a medical odyssey, and my partner in this during the most crucial part of my journey has been my neurologist, Dr Stephen Tisch. I thank him for his ongoing exceptional care and treatment.

I am deeply appreciative of my wonderful team of carers: my Personal Assistant, Ron Compagnucci, who has consistently offered off-the-chart support, willing to assist on any and all occasions and always with the greatest of sensitivity.

Kristina Rajbhandari, Dawn Sunga, Jyobina Pikha, Jackina Rajbhandari, Frankie Shires and the aforementioned Ron and Natalie, have helped carry me through the day-to-day and night-to-night minutiae of my disease with the utmost warmth and patience. I could not have lived the life I continue to live without them. To my long-time friend, Dr Tony Lowy, I am deeply grateful for your loyal support.

Gratitude goes to the many specialists who have been critical in maintaining my quality of life as I battle Parkinson's: my speech therapists Kristin Arthur, Betsy Rumble and Jennifer Stacy; physiotherapists Katie Hillier, Becky Martin, Frances Elizabeth McKirdy and Courtney Raman; personal trainer Neil Harris; drumming teacher Tomer Aloni; art therapist Anna Barten; and massage therapists Henrietta Winn and Kimberley Morrissey. I am indebted to my long-term psychotherapist Margaret Berkovic, whose understanding of the human condition has enabled me to see my situation from perspectives otherwise inaccessible to me.

Finally, at the foundation of everything, is family.

To my brother Ron, whose support I know I can count on, I give thanks. To my wife, Gene, who has been steadfastly by my side for more than half a century – my beloved lifelong companion, my inspiration in life and work, and, in recent years, my safe harbour in a sea of turmoil. I am grateful beyond words for your enduring, unconditional love and care. I cannot imagine my life without you. To my children Emile and Ondine, daughter-in-law Caroline and son-in-law Dror, and my six grandchildren – Milo, Zachary, Cy, Jasmine, Dov and Lev – together and individually, your presence in my life, whether near or separated from me by oceans, enables me to keep going. Even as my broader horizons diminish, your loving presence fills my life with meaning. You are the balm that soothes the harsh winter of my days.

With all my love, I dedicate this book to each and every one you.

About the Author

BRIAN SHERMAN AM has enjoyed a distinguished career in business as Chair and Joint Managing Director of the EquitiLink Group, from its inception in 1981 to December 2000. EquitiLink was one of the largest independent funds management groups in Australia, with $6 billion in funds under management. Throughout his career, Brian has been President and Director of a number of investment companies listed on the American and Canadian stock exchanges, and was Chair of Aberdeen Leaders Limited (listed). Brian was also Chair of Finance and a board member of the 2000 Sydney Organising Committee for the Olympic Games (SOCOG). He was President of the Australian Museum Trust from 2001 to 2009, and Director of Network Ten from 1994 to 2007.

With his daughter Ondine, Brian is the co-founder and co-managing director of Voiceless, an organisation which has, since 2004, been at the forefront internationally of the animal protection and animal law movements since 2004.

In 2010, Brian was awarded an honorary Doctorate of Letters from the University of Technology Sydney in recognition of his outstanding contribution to the advancement of society in Australia and overseas. He was appointed a member of the Order of Australia in 2004 for his service to the community as a philanthropist and benefactor to arts, education and sporting organisations, and to business and commerce. Brian is also the recipient of an Ernst & Young Entrepreneur of the Year award. His memoir, *The Lives of Brian*, written with AM Jonson, was published in 2018.